If I Die,

Will They Ever Believe

Jesus Heals?

By

Sarah Jane Lavery

Cover photos by: Sarah Jane Lavery and Kelly Moore Dunn
Cover design by Geoffrey F. Tarr
Edited by Geoffrey F. Tarr

Printed in the United States of America

First Edition, 2017

Editions	2017		2018		2019		2020		2021		2022		2023		2024		2025		2026		2027		2028	
	1	7	1	7	1	7	1	7	1	7	1	7	1	7	1	7	1	7	1	7	1	7	1	7
	2	8	2	8	2	8	2	8	2	8	2	8	2	8	2	8	2	8	2	8	2	8	2	8
	3	9	3	9	3	9	3	9	3	9	3	9	3	9	3	9	3	9	3	9	3	9	3	9
	4	10	4	10	4	10	4	10	4	10	4	10	4	10	4	10	4	10	4	10	4	10	4	10
	5	11	5	11	5	11	5	11	5	11	5	11	5	11	5	11	5	11	5	11	5	11	5	11
	6	12	6	12	6	12	6	12	6	12	6	12	6	12	6	12	6	12	6	12	6	12	6	12

ISBN-13: 978-0-9986331-0-7
ISBN-10: 0-9986331-0-0

Quotes

The inspiring story of a mother's indomitable faith as she faces illness, persecution and death. Like Job, Sarah Jane refuses to capitulate to the cynical forces around her and keeps her eyes fixed on Jesus. Wonderful example for any parent who may be facing difficulties. Never give up!
Fr. Marc R. Montminy, Exeter, New Hampshire - Pastor, St. Michael's Parish; Leader in New Hampshire Charismatic Renewal; Vlogger

This book is a marvelous testament of the deepest faith in Jesus. Faced with life-threatening adversity Sarah Jane and her daughter Mari-Beth continue to praise God and trust him in every situation. A most inspiring read!
Susan Stanford-Rue, PhD, Jacksonville, Florida - Psychologist; Counselor; Author

This very personal and inspiring account of the triumph of love over death will help people realize that if they believe in Him, Jesus always heals—sometimes bodies and always spirits! Even though Mari-Beth was not physically healed, many spirits were healed through her journey and faith. Sarah Jane has kept her promise to Mari-Beth to tell everyone that Jesus always heals!
Sister Mary Rose Reddy, DMML, Rochester, New Hampshire – St. Charles Children's Home; Director of Family Faith Formation at Our Lady of the Holy Rosary and St. Leo Parishes; Author; Blogger

Dedication

My daughters, The Moore girls

In order as they appear top to bottom, left to right

Kimberly Ann Moore Kunkel, Mari-Beth Moore Barrett,

Kelly Maureen Moore Dunn, Teresa Marie Moore Tarr

Meghan Mary Moore Vasil

Acknowledgements

† I give thanks to The Holy Family, my family and all the family of God who have become a part of our story

† My heartfelt gratitude to my daughter Kimberly Ann for her willingness to relive her journey and courageously share her story in this book

† Special thanks to Dennis Tompkins for his remembrance of Mari-Beth and for sharing his faith

† Thank you to my editor Geoffrey F. Tarr and to Teresa M. Tarr, Sister Mary Rose DMML and Mary McDonnell for their assistance in editing.

† Prayerful gratitude to Rev. Marc R. Montminy, St. Michael Parish, Exeter, NH, Susan Stanford-Rue, PhD, Jacksonville, FL and Sister Mary Rose, DMML, St. Charles Children's Home, Rochester, NH

† Special thanks to my family for all their encouragement and prayerful support, especially to Geoffrey F. and Teresa M. Tarr for all their help.

Table of Contents

Introduction

Life teaches us many valuable lessons through our everyday experiences. Wisdom and prudence encourage us to be open-minded and accessible enough to learn from the gift of our daily lives including from those with whom we live. I have learned a great deal from the five daughters God gave me and continue to learn through them as well as from my grandchildren.

This book is inspired by my daughter Mari-Beth, who lived life in the beauty of God's grace that uttered simple desires, to love and be loved. She loved God and loved her life, living it the way many are still living and died as many are still dying. Mari-Beth believed God heals and she enjoyed many experiences of consolation and healing and struggled through times of desolation during her battle with the cancer that ultimately took her life.

However, her greatest suffering was not the cancer that ravaged her young body; it was enduring the unbelief of those around her. Her frustration at this unbelief disturbed and grieved her almost to the point of desperation at times.

In one of those moments, she said, "Mom, I believe that Jesus can heal me here on earth or take me to heaven. Because I truly believe this, they (referring to her medical caregivers as well as many family and friends) all think I'm crazy now. If I die, how will they ever believe Jesus heals? Who will tell them?"

My answer was as simple as her question as I responded, without hesitation, "We will", Mari-Beth. Your sisters and I will tell them by the witness of our lives."

I think her question was really directed to those around her that doubted; some family, friends and the medical personnel that she encountered, not necessarily to the whole world. My spontaneous response was simple and sincere but I had no idea how that statement would impact my future. Hindsight may be 20/20 but foresight is definitely shrouded.

Soon after Mari-Beth died, I began to journal my experiences regarding Mari-Beth's death. Journaling my feelings and thoughts, I believe helped me to grieve this unspeakable loss of my beautiful 26 year old daughter. It consoled me to remember how God was with us; how God walked us through the darkness, always providing His light. I wanted to remember this amazing daughter who so loved God and showed it in her gentle unassuming way to everyone even to the end of her life. Mari-Beth often said, "Mom, when Jesus heals me, we will write a book to glorify God and go on the road telling everyone that Jesus heals."

After 32 years, it is time to share our story; it is important to share on so many levels. It is a simple, honest revelation of how Mari-Beth's life impacted our entire family. How her death spurred me on to tell the story of how Jesus Christ heals and how Jesus loves each one of us. It is my hope that this book will be a blessing to all that "happen" to read it, especially to my family and friends.

There are some who never had an opportunity to know Mari-Beth, the beautiful loving woman she became, and the incredibly courageous way she carried her cross, always looking to the resurrection, praising the Lord to the last moment of her life.

Since 1984, the medical advances in cancer treatments have been phenomenal. Many of our medical centers treat the whole person: spiritually, emotionally, and physically. Now, there is a wide recognition that spiritual healing often enhances physical healing. There is now a greater respect for the patient's choices regarding treatment with an emphasis for more information so the patient may make informed choices on which treatment plan meets their needs. My Mari-Beth would have had such a vastly different experience and perhaps, a more favorable outcome if she was treated today.

I do believe God reveals to us many amazing truths in life that may only be learned through experience. Only in His grace do we have the courage to share the experience. In doing so, it is my profound hope that this writing may have merit and glorify God as well as she did.

I
Spring 1984

*Watch and pray that you may
not undergo the test.
The spirit is willing,
but the flesh is weak.*

Mt. 26:41

Suddenly I awoke from a sound sleep with a sharp pain in my chest. As I attempted to sit up, I realized that my left arm was numb. Pushing with my right hand, I managed to sit up on the side of the bed. Frightened, I began praying in tongues (my prayer language) and slowly felt my body calming down. Noting that my breathing and pulse were normal, I thought, "why this pain if there is nothing wrong with me?" Then I thought of my daughter, Mari-Beth who was two weeks overdue for the birth of their first child. I woke Tom up and asked him to pray with me.

The previous evening, we received a call from my son-in-law, Dan. Mari-Beth finally started labor and they had made the hour long trip from Newark, NY to the Rochester, NY hospital. Unfortunately, after they got there, Mari-Beth wanted to return home because the labor pains had stopped. Dan asked me to talk to her, hoping that I would help to convince her to stay in the hospital overnight. Sometimes the fact that I am a nurse carries a little more weight with my family when just being a mother isn't quite enough. After we talked, she agreed to stay in the hospital overnight and reassess the situation in the morning.

"Perhaps she has started labor again and needs prayer," I thought. Maybe this pain was a wake-up call to intercede, I reasoned. We prayed and prayed and finally Tom fell asleep praying. Although my pain persisted, I didn't have the heart to wake him up again. I knew he needed to rise early to go to Niagara University in Buffalo, NY to pick up my youngest daughter Meghan, who was coming home for her summer break from college.

I went into Teresa's room and woke her up to pray. Teresa is the fourth of my five daughters. She had graduated from Steubenville University (now Franciscan University), located in Ohio, the week before and just arrived home. I explained my need to her and she was very willing to pray. However, after praying for a few minutes, she too fell asleep.

Still in pain, I went into the spare bedroom and continued to pray by myself. As I prayed, I heard the Lord say, "Don't be discouraged, I'm with you".
Then I said, "Now I know how you must have felt, Lord, when you asked the disciples to pray one hour with you as you agonized in the garden of Gethsemane and they all fell asleep." I continued to pray.

Soon it was morning. Tom poked his head in through the doorway that was slightly ajar and asked if I was alright. I nodded, "Go ahead, I'll be fine". It's a long drive to Niagara

University from Utica and I didn't want to delay his departure.

I prayed and dozed, prayed and dozed, never really sleeping and still in pain. Around 10:30AM I thought, "Enough praying!" I decided to go to Mass. There was a noon Mass at a church downtown near my office that I often attended. I got up quickly, showered and dressed and was on my way.

Still in some pain, I considered that I may need Confession. As I was praying, I searched my conscience for any "blocks that may hinder healing". "Suppose there was something in me that needed healing. If I needed a healing touch from the Lord for this pain, was there anything in me that could block healing?" My thoughts were racing.

I thought of the events of the past week that disturbed me. There was the letter from our pastor forbidding me to use the gifts of the Spirit or come to the prayer meeting. The whole scenario surrounding the letter was strange. To explain the events, seems even stranger.

Tom and I were married on March 16, 1984 and we were actively involved in a parish that was vibrant with the power of the Holy Spirit with a growing prayer meeting. God was using me powerfully in the prophetic and healing gifts in the prayer meeting and in our healing Masses.

Things seemed to be falling into place for me after many years of single parenting. My youngest daughter was still in college but the other four girls each appeared to be successfully making their way in life.

I was still very busy working full time as a social worker for the County Social Services, where I had been for the past eighteen years. One day, during an interview, the client named Mary shared some very intimate details with me that seemed a bit strange since this was a one-time interview that really involved an employment situation. (I always wore a cross which is a silent witness to my faith). She indicated that she needed to see a priest and asked my help. I told her of the church across the street where she could inquire. She asked if I would make the call for her. So I did. I called the priest from that parish (who was actually my spiritual director) and made an appointment for her for 1:00 PM that day. Mary thanked me and left.

Moments later, while I was way from my desk, a co-worker took a message for me from Mary saying she could not keep the appointment with Father Mike. I quickly called Father Mike to cancel the appointment that he was so gracious to give her. Interestingly enough, while Father Mike and I were talking he put me on hold to take another call. When he came back on the line, he said, "That was Father (my pastor) on the other line. When I told him that I had you on hold, he asked if you were calling about the letter. I told him you had called for something else. Did you get a letter from him?"

"Not that I know of. But I'll call home and have Teresa check the mail. I don't have a very good feeling about this, Father. Since my client cancelled, would you see me instead?

"Yes, I'll be here."

"I'll take personal leave with my lunch time and come directly."

Meanwhile, I called Teresa at home. "Teresa, please check the mail to see if there is a letter for me from our parish. I'll hold on while you check."

"I'm back, Mom. There is a letter for you from the parish. Do you want me to open it and read it to you?"

"No thanks, Teresa. But would you mind taking the letter to Father Mike right now. Just give it to him. He'll understand. I have an appointment with him at 1:00 PM."

"Okay, Mom"

"Thanks, Tre, I really appreciate it. Bye."

When I met with Father Mike, He said, "Teresa brought me the letter, do you want to open it?"

"No, Father, you open it and read it first. Then I'll read it. My heart's been pounding making me feel like this is not a good sign. First, let me tell you about Teresa's graduation from Steubenville University (now Franciscan University) last weekend. We are so proud of her."

After filling him in on all the details, I said "Now the letter, Father. He opened the letter and read it. As he handed it to me, he said, "It says in this letter that he discussed this with me before making this decision. That is not true. Today while we were on the phone and I put you on hold was the only time I heard this from him."

As I read the letter. I didn't know whether to laugh or cry. It was all about forbidding me to use the charismatic gifts in the community and questioning where I had been the last few weeks. "So, apparently he lied about talking to you first, right?" "Apparently". "What do you think you should do?" Father Mike asked.
"Well, it seems pretty ridiculous for him to question where I've been lately since we did go away on a honeymoon and to Ohio for graduation, but we've been in church in between and it has only been a matter of a few weeks. I don't really get it but I'll be quiet for awhile if that's what he wants. I'll just shut-up and have a vacation from speaking!"
"You're OK with that?"
"Yes, of course. What else can I do? He's the pastor."

"Good for you."

As I was leaving, I turned to Father and said, "Isn't it a strange sequence of events? While doing my job and minding my own business and trying to help someone else God led me here to you today?" He smiled and agreed.

"I'm glad that you read the letter first. I'm grateful that God protects me as he always promised. It's too bad he had to lie about it all but I'm glad to know the truth. Thank you so much, Father. Bye."

I left the rectory with mixed emotions. On the one hand, I felt totally rejected and betrayed by my own pastor. On the other hand, I felt affirmed and encouraged by my spiritual director and truly protected by God. To think that I was blessed to have Father Mike read the letter first was amazing to me.

.

Returning to my office, I took the letter out and read it again. It really was ludicrous. I could tell someone else was part of this. It was a poorly written letter with mistakes in it plus the fact that it quoted a lie. However, it was the pastor's signature so I would have to accept it and live with it. I knew I would forgive it and go on. It's no big deal. I had other responsibilities more pressing. So I thought I was okay.

Here's an interesting question in hindsight. "Who was that young girl Mary and where did she disappear to?" I never did see her again and would not recognize her now if I did. Was she a real person or an angel sent to protect me once again?"

If Father wanted to silence me, I'd just be quiet. But had I forgiven him? I thought so but maybe I hadn't. I needed to be sure I allowed no blocks to healing in my being. I learned that lesson a long time ago. No matter what the situation, I knew that with the Sacrament of Reconciliation, I could forgive anything. So that was my plan. I would take it to Confession.

Confession was at 11:30 and Mass at 12:10 so this was perfect timing. I don't know if the priest understood what I was confessing or not but he listened patiently, gave me my penance and absolution and I felt better. Although the chest pain was still present, it was reduced to a dull ache. I stayed for Mass and received Holy Communion asking the Lord to heal me and to be with Mari-Beth.

II
A New Life is Born

*I came so that they might have life
and have it more abundantly.*

John 10:10b

W hen I arrived home, there was a message waiting for me. Emily Mari Barrett was born at 10:30AM. It was Saturday, May 19, 1984. All was well, Praise the Lord! (Note - the chest pain did not leave until the end of the day).

We were very excited to go to Rochester the very next day to see my beautiful new granddaughter. This was my second grandchild but a new experience for me. My oldest grandchild, Joshua David Kunkel was born in Colorado and I was not able to see him until he was eight months old. This time I would be able to hold this brand new life that was - "just one day out of heaven". What a blessing it was for me. Holding little Emily Mari was like holding Mari-Beth all over again. She was so sweet with her little round face, blue eyes and tiny nose. Another miracle! God had done it again. We were all thrilled.

Before we left, Mari-Beth asked me if I would come to Newark the following day because the doctor wanted to do some tests regarding a lump in her arm that she had discovered months before. I agreed. But my heart fell.

My thoughts went back to that fateful day. I had tried to put this out of my mind and prayed that I did not hear God clearly months before when she first discovered the lump. Mari-Beth was about 4 or 5 months pregnant. She had called me and told me that she wasn't feeling well and decided to stay home from work. She was a Speech Pathologist working with children which she dearly loved. It was a Friday and she thought if she had a long weekend she could rest up and forestall any virus or whatever germ might be brewing in her system. As she was taking a shower, she discovered a lump in the inner aspect of her right elbow. As we talked, I felt a chill go through my body and felt sick as I heard in my spirit

"its cancer". Without revealing this word to her I said, "Mari-Beth, you need to call your doctor and see him immediately". She agreed and hung up.

Awhile later, she called back and said the doctor couldn't see her, that he was booked till her next appointment. I was furious. I said, "Mari-Beth, you need to call Dan (her husband) and get dressed and just go anyway. Call your doctor and tell him you're coming in and insist that someone see you." I don't know what was said but she did get to see the doctor. The doctor treated it very lightly and referred her to a neurologist in Rochester. There she was told "it's just a simple neuroma that can be taken care of after the baby is born". Relieved with this diagnosis, I accepted the fact that I must have been wrong in what I heard in my spirit and I let it go with great relief. I thought the threat was over.

16

There were times during the following months that she had pain in her arm that really disturbed her. We thought that was normal and that it was pressing on a nerve causing pain. Sometimes she would call me on the phone for prayer. I can remember praying the Psalms and praying in tongues over the phone until she could sleep. She accepted that this would all be taken care of after the birth of her child and she would be well once again.

Now here it was again and I had to face it with her. The doctors now decided it looked suspicious and ordered a biopsy. Three days after Emily was born, the biopsy was done and she was diagnosed with Embryno-rhabdo-myosarcoma, a fast growing cancer that usually appears in the immature muscle in children – very rare in adults.

When the doctor came to the bedside to speak to her about her test results, he seemed evasive. I began to grow impatient and I said, "She needs to know the truth."
He responded, "I don't know if she can take it now."
"If it's the truth, she can take it"
Mari-Beth nodded, "I need to know".
He then proceeded with the diagnosis and the prognosis which was grim to say the least. The treatment available offered no hope of a cure. They suggested amputation of her right arm,

chemotherapy and radiation or all three. The best she could expect would be that she would live less than a year, with or without treatment.

To say that the shock in the room was overwhelming is an understatement. Dan, who was standing at the head of the bed next to her turned gray and began to slide down the wall in back of the bed. As he did, Mari-Beth motioned to reach toward him, then looked at me and said, "Mom?" – as if there was something I could do. At that moment, without hesitation, I reached over and placed my hand on Mari-Beth, and in direct eye contact with the doctor standing on the opposite site of the bed, I said, "Jesus Christ is the same today as he was yesterday and will be tomorrow. He will tell us what to do." (Consciously, I had never uttered that Scripture before. In fact, I wasn't aware that I knew it until that moment).

I don't know what the doctor thought. He wasn't a Christian to my knowledge but it didn't matter to me. I wasn't trying to impress anyone. I truly believed God was with us but the shock was indescribable.

Dan was devastated and I encouraged him to tell his family even though I knew it would be difficult. I knew he would need their prayer and support. I also encouraged him to stay close to the sacraments and if he had any unforgiveness in his life to get rid of it with the help of the Sacrament of Reconciliation. He admitted that the only person he had trouble forgiving was Mari-Beth's father for his neglect of our family. I remember saying, "I forgave him years ago. You need to do the same. We're asking BIG - We need a miracle and you need God's peace! You don't want any obstacles in the way."

I didn't know that much about healing at that point. Healing Ministry was still pretty new in my life, comparatively speaking. However, I believed that there can be obstacles to healing caused by things like an unforgiving heart and unbelief. I'm certain he brought everything to the Lord and I never mentioned it again. Life totally changed for all of us that day.

III
Looking Backward

Look back – but don't stare

Our life was fairly simple as the girls grew up. It was a real challenge raising five daughters as a single Mom. I was able to support them on my meager social worker salary. I was adamant about educating them in Catholic schools and we struggled to accomplish it, whatever it took. My strong faith always reminded me that God would take care of us and He did.

Their father did not support us or participate in their lives. He was somewhere in Florida, still suffering from the disease of alcoholism. We were actively involved in the Al-Anon program. We accepted our lives without him and were a pretty happy family, all very close to one another.

Mari-Beth was the second of the five Moore girls. When I went into labor for her birth twelve days early, I was in a difficult place emotionally. I had just learned some disturbing news. My brother David's wife, Mimi had just given birth to their third child who was born prematurely. The baby was doing fine. However, they learned that their oldest son Davey, almost 3 years old, was diagnosed with acute lymphatic leukemia.

In those days, no one ever talked about prayers for healing. We believed that God could do miracles but did He want to? No one expected that He would unless one could travel to a holy place like Lourdes, France, where healing miracles had been reported. Options for treatment were limited and basically not successful for this leukemia. So if medical science could not take care of it, there was no hope for him.

I had a hard time accepting the fact that this little boy who was so loved and seemed so healthy could become fatally ill in a few weeks! He only had a sore throat. That happens to children all the time, doesn't it? They get sore throats and are treated and get well. It doesn't turn into leukemia! How could this be happening? All my family lived in Oswego, which was about three hours away. I felt so helpless and so far away. No matter how I cried out to God, it seemed there was no answer.

Interestingly, during the long difficult labor, I had held a rosary in my hand through the entire labor and delivery so tightly that I had the imprint of the cross in my hand all the next day. Mari-Beth was born on June 9, 1958. She was a beautiful, healthy blue-eyed baby girl. She had round face with delicate features and a perfectly round head with curls already. She was 6lbs. 1 ½ oz, a bit small but her birth was a bit early. Perfectly perfect!

Mari-Beth wasn't actually due to be born until June 21, 1958, which strangely enough turned out to be the day Davey died. I remember it so well. I had spent a terrible night. Mari-Beth was such an easy baby but she had to be fed every three hours which was no problem normally. However, on this particular night, she would not eat and she fussed all night. I became so stressed and filled with anxiety, I couldn't rest either. Finally, about 5:00 AM, we both quieted down and fell asleep. The phone rang at 7:00 AM and I nudged her father to answer it saying, "I can't answer that. It's my brother calling to tell us that Davey died." I could hardly believe I said that. He had only been sick only a matter of a few weeks. How could this be happening?

To make matters worse for me, I couldn't attend the wake and the funeral. My left leg was so swollen; I couldn't even wear a shoe and definitely couldn't travel. The doctor said I must have injured it during labor. It was so hard to just let Ralph go without me. My only choice was to simply accept it all, just as it was.

Mari-Beth was a sweet delicate child, beautiful with her big blue eyes and curly hair. She was always very active, loved to swim and ride her bike. She graduated from Our Lady of Lourdes Catholic Elementary School, Utica Catholic Academy for Girls and St. Rose College in Albany, NY. She was baptized in the Holy Spirit, loved the scriptures, had a wonderful gift of prayer and was very devoted to Our Blessed Mother.

She always got along well with her friends. She had a happy outlook on everything. That was her nature; gentle and caring and basically pretty happy and peaceful. She loved helping people, especially children. She participated in the Louise DeMerillac Society after school, helping children learn to read. During one of her summer jobs while in High School, she worked at the Association for Retarded Children and fell in love with those children with Down Syndrome. She gave me few, if any, anxious moments growing up, even in the teen years! Her sisters always referred to her as "the perfect one". That was their way of teasing her especially when she tried to keep them out of trouble. Raising girls is pretty interesting, especially when they try to "mother" each other.

Mari-Beth met Dan Barrett while she was in college at St. Rose in Albany, NY and he was at Albany Law School. I liked him from the start. I was happy to know that his Catholic faith is important to him. I knew it would be important to her as well. Her sisters all loved him too which was an extra bonus for Mari-Beth. In her senior year, they were engaged. They seemed well suited to each other – the perfect couple.

Planning Mari-Beth's wedding was a string of divine

appointments. Everything fell into place so easily. Since she was in college in Albany and we lived in Utica, it meant she had to come home to plan and shop. In typical fashion, believing God can do anything, she called and told me she had one day in which to accomplish it all.

She and Dan had already talked to Father and engaged the church and reserved the place for the reception. I put all my doubts aside and agreed. I told her I had to attend a conference that morning until 10:00 AM but would be available for 10:30 AM.

We prayed, picked a bridal shop out of the phone book and started there. By 12:30 PM, she had chosen her dress and was working on the veil. I checked my watch and suggested that we could make it to 1:00 PM Mass at St. Francis de Sales Church, grab lunch on the way back and continue the shopping. She agreed and we told the saleslady we would be back.

At Mass, during the prayer of the faithful, we thanked the Lord for our progress and asked help to finish all the details. We returned to the bridal shop and she chose the veil from the seven she tried on (it looked just like her First Communion veil). We also picked out the bridesmaids dresses and bought my dress. From there, we went on to engage the florist, choose the invitations and thank you notes and even ordered the cake. Arriving home for dinner, we were so happy. God did it for us in one day. Now she could return to school at peace, knowing all was in order in plenty of time.

They were married on July 12, 1980, with Father Kenneth Doyle (Dan's friend) and Father Francis Pompei celebrating the ceremony at St. Francis DeSales Church in Utica, NY. It was a beautiful wedding. Mari-Beth wanted everything in blue to honor Our Lady; pale blue for the attendants dresses, navy blue for the men and even I wore blue. She put tiny rosaries in each bouquet. We prayed through every detail. There was no detail too small to pray about. The results were incredible.

One of the musical selections she chose for the ceremony was a wonderful new song, "Hail Mary, Gentle Woman". She even chose the soloist at a prayer meeting. One night after a prayer meeting she said, "Mom, I met a young woman tonight at the prayer meeting and asked her to sing at my wedding and she said yes."
I was astonished and a bit doubtful. "How do you know she can sing?" I asked. "Have you ever heard her sing?"
"Well, I was next to her in the prayer meeting when we were praising the Lord", She replied.
"How can you be sure, if that's all you heard?"

With a big smile she answered, "Oh, I asked the Lord and He said that she was the one I should ask". That was it. She had no doubt.

When I heard this young woman sing at the wedding, I was amazed. She had a beautiful, incredibly powerful, outstanding soprano voice. I was moved to tears. It was wonderful.

As they grew in their marriage, Mari-Beth and Dan developed a beautiful prayer relationship and prayed about everything. Dan had settled into his position in the family law firm with his brother and father. Mari-Beth began working on her master's degree at Geneseo SUNY. Dan was a great encouragement to her, even helping her to study. She achieved her degree with flying colors and began her career as a speech pathologist.

An interesting thing happened after they had been married only a couple of weeks. She called to ask my advice. She said that she and Dan were not in agreement on a particular thing. It seems that they had two invitations for the same day and couldn't agree on which one to attend. She said, "Mom, we have never had a serious disagreement and I certainly don't want to have one over this." So I suggested she might want to try something I was learning to do. I suggested that they do this over a period of three days before they decide. The first day, they should pray together and then separately make a list of all the pros regarding their individual choice and surrender it to the Lord. The second day, use the same procedure for the cons. Then the third day, pray and ask the Lord for the answer. So she agreed that it was worth a try.

Three days later, she called me all excited, in the middle of the day while I was at the office "Mom, sorry for calling you at work but I just couldn't wait to tell you what happened. We did what you suggested but didn't seem to get the answer yet. So when Dan left for the office this morning, I knelt down by the bedside to pray and listen a little longer.

I heard the Lord say, "Mari-Beth, do you want the gift of tongues?" and I felt a pounding in my chest. I answered yes and was "overpowered with the Spirit" on my bed. I woke up "praying in tongues" and heard the Lord's answer to me – "Let your husband have his choice; do whatever he chooses". So I called Dan immediately. He told me that the Lord had given him the scripture from Ephesians 5 about wives being subject to husbands but he didn't tell me because he was afraid I might think he was trying to "Lord it over me".

She laughed and said, "I guess God figured I do need the gift of tongues." She was so thrilled!
(When Mari-Beth was baptized in the Holy Spirit some time before this, I asked her if she received the "gift of tongues".

She answered no. When I inquired as to whether or not she had asked the Lord for the gift, she said she didn't think she needed tongues. So I just said okay and let it drop. God is so amazing!)

They bought a home in Newark and waited patiently for their family to begin. They prayed and asked the Lord to give them a child. Mari-Beth so wanted to became a mother. After her older sister Kimberly gave birth to Joshua (my first grandchild), she could talk of nothing else but starting a family. She thought it was taking too long and was beginning to fear she couldn't conceive a child. Even though Dan was not really much interested in the Charismatic prayer meetings, he agreed to go with her to their parish prayer meeting at St. Michael's Church to pray for a child.

Meanwhile, they got a puppy, a golden retriever, and named her Lady Diana. Dan had always had a dog growing up. They were both excited about Lady Di who was born May 19, 1983.

A few months later, they announced that Mari-Beth was pregnant and due in May 1984. Their prayers had been answered and they were so very happy. Mari-Beth was pretty healthy throughout her pregnancy. She was careful to eat healthy, never was a smoker or drinker, exercised and liked to run. She enjoyed her job and absolutely loved the children she worked with. Happily anticipating the birth of their first child, things couldn't look better, as far as she was concerned, except for the pain in her arm. She totally trusted it would be taken care of just as the doctors told her.

Our home was an all female household until I married Tom on March 16, 1984. One of the most significant things about this wedding ceremony involved Mari-Beth. She was seven months pregnant and had found a dress she was excited about that she wanted to wear to the wedding. It was a beautiful red taffeta dress with long sleeves and straight lines that wasn't even a maternity dress that looked great on her. She was concerned about the color and how I would feel about her wearing red, since it wouldn't match anyone else. She looked beautiful in it with her white stockings and her black low-heeled pumps. I told her I loved it and she was pleased. She read from the Book of Revelation at the wedding. Sometimes I remember this and think of the significance of her wearing red and reading from the Wedding of the Lamb proclaiming "Alleluia" from the altar. It was the last time she would ever be dressed so beautifully and share with us in this church... On the next March 16th she would be truly attending the banquet in eternity.

At this point in time, I thought the job of raising the family was almost done or at least in transition. The nest was almost empty. Kimberly Ann, the oldest, was married to Lee Kunkel and lived in Colorado with their son Joshua. Kelly, third in line, and Mari-Beth's best friend was married to Peter Dunn and they lived in Manchester NH. Peter was also a long time close friend of Mari-Beth's. She loved the fact that they were both her best friends and that they married and she felt like she was partly responsible for that match. For years, Kelly and Peter had a quote on their refrigerator that reads, "First you meet a beautiful girl, then she introduces you to her younger sister!"

Teresa had just graduated from Steubenville University on May 12, 1984 and was anticipating a job teaching Music in three Catholic Schools: Tupper Lake, Lake Placid and Saranac Lake, NY. Meghan was finishing her sophomore year at Niagara University. Life was changing and I was ready to focus on being a wife again, a mother-in-law and a grandmother. Little did I know what was in store. Nothing would ever be the same for any of us.

IV
The Journey Begins

Jesus Christ is the same
yesterday, today, and forever.
Hebrews 13:8

How would she ever be able to face all of this? She was only three days post-partum with this newborn baby to care for. Since that they had done the biopsy in her right arm, she was truly limited in what she could do. When she asked me to come and stay with her, I could hardly refuse but I had to consider Tom and our marriage. I trusted God would show the way.

I returned to Utica to talk to Tom and pray about this. Tom and I had been good friends for years long before we were married on March 16, 1984. He became very attached to my daughters over the years and was very receptive to my going to help her; in fact, he encouraged me. I knew our marriage was very new and it would be a challenge but I felt that as long as I had his blessing, it was God's plan. We agreed that Newark was only two hours away and we would have weekends. I was granted a medical leave of absence from my social work position with no problem. My spiritual director Father Mike prayed with me before I left. I said, "Father, I am grateful that God has used me in healing and prophecy in our community, but what good am I if He can't use me for my own family?" He understood. I went to Newark with Tom's blessing as well as Father Mike's. I knew I was supported and felt I was doing the right thing.

Dan knew that there were more gifts of the Holy Spirit for him to experience and now he wanted them all. He had witnessed them in others, especially through Mari-Beth and the people at the prayer meeting. He had never been prayed with for the Baptism in the Holy Spirit (the release or manifestations of the gifts of the Holy Spirit that are actually given at confirmation). When we prayed with him, God began to manifest many of the gifts in his life; tongues, prophecy, thirst for the scriptures, etc. I knew the gifts would be a source of strength and wisdom for him. God is so generous to us.

Mari-Beth grappled with the whole idea of taking a treatment that was very aggressive even though it was not expected to be effective against this cancer. She listened to all the advice given by the consultants called in. They had nothing more to offer. She wanted to leave it all up to the Lord. She talked about The City of Faith Hospital at Oral Roberts University in Tulsa, Oklahoma. She knew that they believed in combining medicine with prayer. She wanted to go there because she knew that without a miracle she would die.

She struggled to make sense of what was happening to her. The questions were overwhelming. How could she take care of Emily with her left arm now that her right arm was pretty much disabled? Should she take treatment? Could she nurse Emily and not take treatment? The doctors were pressuring her to begin treatment as if there was no time to lose. She wanted time to pray it through but no one wanted to wait for her decision. Dan and his family were in panic-mode – like – get started already, there's no time to waste. She had waited all this time for the doctors to move and now everyone wanted her to hurry up and make a decision and begin treatment immediately.

It was pretty frustrating and extremely painful to watch. As her mother, I knew she needed time but I had to keep quiet and let it all unfold. I prayed without ceasing for God to show her the way. I tried to stay in the background as much as possible but she wanted me there. I reassured her that no matter what she chose to do, I would be there for her and support her totally, regardless of her choices. I would soon learn that this would not be easy for her, Dan, me nor the rest of the family.

I had no lofty goals when I decided to stay with Mari-Beth and help. It was for one reason alone. That was because she asked me if I would stay with her until she was healed – one way or the other. She knew well what the prognosis was and she wanted me there. As long as Dan welcomed me and I had Tom's blessing, it didn't matter to me what anyone else thought.

I persevered as prayerfully and quietly as I could. I got up every day at the crack of dawn, spent my hour with the Lord, showered, dressed, and went to morning Mass. When I returned Dan was ready to leave for the office and I became the caregiver. I took care of Emily and did whatever household chores needed doing and helped Mari-Beth with personal care. Dan was great about doing things when he was at home. He also did all the grocery shopping. We got along very well. We were like the right and the left hand working together. It seemed to be working fine.

I was with her as she began the chemotherapy; three aggressive drugs were administered intravenously. She was disturbed that with every treatment, they reviewed the side-effects all over again. Voicing her annoyance, she would say, "Why do they do that? I've signed the permission slip, I know the side effects. I just finish praying away the negative thoughts in my mind and they remind me all over again". I had no answers. I just prayed.

The chemotherapy made her violently ill. Her retching turned me inside out. I couldn't even imagine what it was doing to her. During one visit, the nurse approached her about a drug, a derivative of marijuana that was available to her, with her signed permission. She was appalled. "Mom, if I have to take this treatment, I won't to be able to praise the Lord and pray. I don't want to behave like a druggie or be laughing like a hyena. That's not for me. Besides, it's totally experimental. They don't even know if it works."Once again, I just had to say, "It's got to be your decision, whatever you decide will be fine with me".

V

Time-out for Renewal

Do not conform yourselves to this age
but be transformed by the renewal of your mind,
that you may discern what is
the will of God, what is good
and pleasing and perfect.

Romans 12:2

I had attended Steubenville Bible Institute's two week long summer sessions for the past few years while Teresa was a student there. I loved it and I learned so much. I even earned continuing education credits. More importantly, it was the only time that I ever had an opportunity to seriously study the scriptures. The bonus was having an excellent scripture teacher in Father Herb Schneider from the Philippines. I had given up any thought of going that year because of Mari-Beth's situation.

But Mari-Beth would have none of that. She began to experience the spiritual warfare we were in not only because of the cancer but because there was so much opposition to her decisions. Emily was going to be baptized and I did not want to miss that either.

She took me aside and said to me, "Mom, you have to go. I know that it will strengthen you. I believe I heard the Lord say that you are going to need this in the days ahead. Please do it, I need you to be strong enough to stay with me." That was hard to hear coming from her lips just imagining what she was going through already. I pondered it and prayed, still resisting to the point where it was two days into the conference when I finally gave in. I left Newark, NY in the wee hours of the morning and drove to Steubenville University alone. Tom agreed to follow later when he could for at least part of the week. Mari-Beth was right. The months ahead would show me how right she was.

In those days, I always thought if God wanted something done, he would tell the person to do it. I didn't expect that I should have to ask for it. Sometimes, I thought if I asked, it might not be God, it might be my own selfishness. I just expected that our friend Father Francis would hear God and come right away to pray with her for a miracle and he didn't. I was really annoyed but didn't say anything to anyone. During Mass, I noticed a priest on the altar who looked so like Father Francis that I had to look twice to be sure it wasn't him. But it wasn't him! He was "signing the Mass' for the deaf. It startled me. What was God showing me?

One of the things that made Mari-Beth think that God would not ask her to have her arm amputated was the fact that she was a speech pathologist who needed to do sign language with both hands. She said, "Mom, why would God want me to lose my ability to sign when he granted me this profession? I have to trust that He will heal me." I had no answer for that.

Now here I was, looking at this priest thinking how annoyed I was at Father Francis, watching him sign with both of his hands and feeling so grieved about Mari-Beth and her need for a miracle. I heard the Lord say – you need to take your annoyance and anger to confession, perhaps to that priest. "Whoa", I thought, "I've got to think about this."

The next day during our morning praise session, that same priest was sitting near me. There was very little time allowed for prophecy on this particular morning. I heard the Lord say, "That priest had a prophecy but time did not allow him to share it. Ask him about it". By this time in my spiritual journey, I had learned to spare myself the pain of hesitating when the Lord prompts me to do something. As the group moved to break, I approached him and said, "Excuse me, Father, may I ask you a question? Did you have a prophetic word to share this morning in the praise session?"

He shot me a startled look and said, "How did you know that?" "The Lord told me", I replied.

He handed me the paper he had written on and said, "Read this".

After reading it, I handed it back to him, smiled and said, "Good word, right on; Father, thank you for sharing it." Smiling, he thanked me and as he walked away with his friend, I heard her say, "I told you so. She's a holy woman. She hears God".

I cringed as I thought, "If the friend only knew how I struggle. I am not worthy of that comment".

However, that occurrence was a confirmation for me that I should seek him out to hear my confession. God is so amazing in how He uses everything to our advantage, regardless of how we resist or whatever. Bible Institute was a time of strengthening and renewing for me and I thank God for that time.

VI
Back to Newark

For I am not ashamed of the gospel.
It is the power of God for the salvation
of everyone who believes:
for Jew first, and then Greek.

Romans 1:16

When I returned to Newark, Mari-Beth greeted me looking so forlorn. She had a scarf wrapped around her head. Scarves were not new for Mari-Beth. She had naturally curly hair that she was always trying to force into a smooth hair-do. She would spend forever blow-drying her hair with a large round hair-brush and then tie a scarf around her head until she left the house to make sure her hair would be perfectly smooth. And it always was – perfectly perfect! In college some of her friends jokingly referred to her as *"Mari-Beth, with the damn perfect hair"*. She looked at me in tears and said as she took off the scarf, "Look, Mom, my hair is all gone."

I smiled and took her head in both my hands and kissed the top of her head and said, "Beautiful, just like when you were a baby."

She broke into a laugh and said, "Leave it to you to think of that."

I laughed with her but what I was thinking was, "Thank you, God, that I didn't make her feel worse by my reaction". It broke my heart. I knew how upset she was.

She then related the story of how she lost all of her hair. She knew it had begun to fall out, seeing it collect on her hair brush and seeing all over her pillow in the morning. She went to her hairdresser to get her hair done and as she was getting her hair shampooed, all of her hair fell out in the sink. She was completely bald. Her hairdresser was wonderful to her. Mari-Beth said they both cried. Then her hairdresser reassured her, made arrangements and took Mari-Beth immediately to a shop to help her buy a wig. It was a traumatic experience but God had provided a compassionate and understanding person to help her through the trauma. I was grateful for that too. (Today, patients are duly prepared for this difficult moment and handle it much easier.)

The distress over her taking treatment continued and she decided to stop it. She couldn't reconcile herself to continue to take this treatment that was not going to help and be so violently ill all the time. She felt the quality of the life she had left was being destroyed. She especially wanted to enjoy Emily as much as she could.

One Saturday, we all decided to go to Confession at their parish. Mari-Beth was happy when she saw the priest that was hearing confessions that day because she liked him. When she came out of the confessional, she was in tears. "All he wanted to talk about is that I should take treatment," she cried. Dan was next and he got much the same. Apparently someone in the family besides Dan and Mari-Beth had already talked to the priest about this.

When I went into the confessional and the priest started to talk to me about Mari-Beth and her struggle with the choice over treatment, I was annoyed. After all, I had come to confess my sins not talk about that.

I said, "Father, isn't it strange? From the time we are able to understand, we are taught that we should depend on God for everything. But when we actually do that, everyone thinks we're nuts!"

"I guess that's true".

That was the end of the discussion. From then on until she died, I took her to Utica to Confession to Father Mike. In fact, he heard her last confession on February 7, 1984, one month before she died.

All she wanted was to take the time to pray and listen to God about what she should do. She knew what everyone else wanted. She wanted to know God's mind on this. The doctors and the family just didn't get it. They thought she was being unreasonable and was ignoring the seriousness of her situation. She knew she would die without a miracle. She simply wanted God to show her what to do about it. Consequently, they began to treat her as a hostile patient, as though she was either crazy or just plain stubborn. They apparently did not understand. They all seemed to forget that it was her decision and her life, not theirs or even Dan's. Moreover, they were upset that I

46

supported whatever she and Dan decided without trying to influence them. Little did I know that they saw me as an obstacle.

During one of her visits to the Cancer Center, her oncologist said to her, "Mari-Beth, I understand that you hear from God."

"Yes, I do, she replied.

Just how does that happen?" he asked.

Smiling with that wide-eyed look of hers, she answered, "Well, I pray, read my scriptures and then I stay quiet. I wait, listening, to hear what the Lord has to say to me."

"Really?" He was incredulous.

"Oh yes, the scripture says, I am the good shepherd, I know my sheep and they know me. They hear my voice and they follow me."

"Well, I don't hear Him like that."

She smiled sweetly at him and said, "Oh, I'm sorry, Doctor, maybe you're not one of His sheep."

At that, he backed up slightly, straightening his back while slightly inflating his chest and said, "Well. I'm a Presbyterian Elder."

She didn't even flinch. Smiling sweetly, she continued, "Well Doctor, I think what you need is the Baptism in the Holy Spirit."

Responding with an incredulous grin, he said, "I don't think we have that in our church."

At that, she turned to me and said, "Mom, do you have any books in your bag?" She knew I always carried spiritual books to read. As it happened I had been reading a book by Agnes Sanford entitled "The Healing Power of the Scriptures".

I reached into my bag, retrieved the book and handed it to the doctor saying, "Here, allow me to make a gift of this to you." Without hesitation, he took the book saying, "I'm going on vacation, and maybe I'll read this".

As we left, Mari-Beth turned to him, still smiling sweetly, and said, "Doctor, if by my next visit, you still haven't experienced the Baptism in the Holy Spirit, I'd be really glad to pray with you for it."

As we left the Center, she was very upbeat. She had an opportunity to witness to her faith and she was very pleased with herself. Of course, I was too. Mostly, I was amazed at the peace and confidence with which she did it and the graciousness with which the doctor accepted it.

VII
A Trip to New Hampshire

Do not be saddened this day,
for rejoicing in the LORD is your strength!

Nehemiah 8:10

In August, she decided that she wanted to go to New Hampshire and visit Kelly and Peter. She thought that we might also attend Father Ralph DiOrio's Healing Service in Worchester, MA. We decided that I would drive her and Emily there in my car. Since Dan had to work, he would pick up Teresa later and meet us in Worchester. Teresa needed healing as well.

In the midst of all this, Teresa had a physical exam and was diagnosed with a tumor of the ovary. She had a second exam and the tumor had grown to nine times its original size. Teresa insisted that she could wait until her health insurance was effective to have the tumor removed. Teresa had just graduated from college which meant she was no longer covered under my health insurance policy. Her teaching job didn't start until September and the insurance coverage would not kick in until January. But I was worried that waiting may be dangerous. What if it was cancer? I couldn't imagine it.

Well, it was a great trip for all of us. We went to the healing service in Worchester. Father Ralph DiOrio had a word of knowledge about an ovarian tumor. Teresa stood up to claim that word. Father called forth people suffering from cancer and Mari-Beth went to sit in the front. It was good for all of us, I thought.

Later, I spoke to Mari-Beth about the service. She was not that encouraged which surprised me because she loved healing services and Masses. She said, "Mom, I wished I hadn't gone up front. I sat near two young girls who were obviously receiving chemotherapy. The Lord spoke to me and told me that their spirits were so broken. I couldn't think of anything else."

On another day, we decided to take a trip to Brookline, MA where our friend, Father Francis Pompei was in formation to become a Franciscan priest. He had left our diocese to join the Franciscans. By this time, I had been healed of being angry with him. We all missed him and looked forward to seeing him. When we greeted him, I told him I was upset with him that he hadn't come to pray with her. I told him the whole story about the priest at Steubenville and said, "I was really angry with you. Then I asked the Lord why you didn't come to pray with her. He said it was because I didn't ask you.

Father said, "Well, you're here now. Let's get to it."

He and Mari-Beth went to the back of the chapel into a confessional. God ministered to them both, I believe.

Mari-Beth said, "I cried. He cried. We both cried. He couldn't believe this was happening to me. He heard my confession and prayed over me. It was great." She was very happy as we departed.

When we returned to Manchester that day, we decided to visit the site where Kelly and Peter were building their first home on Benjamin Street in Manchester. Construction was moving at a snail's pace and they were anxious about the progress. We took some holy water and we all prayed and blessed the hole in the ground that was to be the foundation. Mari-Beth was enjoying every moment. She was convinced that the construction would be stepped up and progress smoothly now that we had prayed.

Since she and Peter were such good friends, she thought nothing of annoying him for a laugh. Peter is very neat and organized about his things. She thought she would pull a prank on him so she enlisted Teresa's help to disorganize his closet while we were there. She thought it was hilarious – Peter? Not so much!

The next day we went shopping at Jordan Marsh (later Macy's) for scarves for Mari-Beth. She had her arm in a sling and carried her arm on a pillow wherever we went. (After having the biopsy done, she was unable to use her right arm and hand). When she signed for her credit card, she wrote with her left hand. I was amazed at how quickly she had learned to write with her left hand. The clerk saw her arm and asked her if she injured it. Mari-Beth said, "Oh, no. I have cancer". As soon as she said it, she saw the stricken look on the clerk's face, smiled and quickly added, "Oooh, it's alright, the Lord Jesus is healing me." The clerk gave a weak smile and nodded.

She shopped for a stroller for Emily. Peter and Kelly took Emily for her first ride in the stroller. There was so much joy when they were all together. I wanted to bottle it and take it back to Newark. It was like a tonic for Mari-Beth, a tonic she so desperately needed that would strengthen her to walk the hard road ahead.

VIII
A Mountain Respite

He said to them, "Come away by yourselves
to a deserted place and rest a while."
People were coming and going
in great numbers, and
they had no opportunity even to eat.

Mark 6:31

As we returned to Newark, Dan and Mari-Beth continued to pray about the treatment. Mari-Beth decided she wanted to get away from Newark and take a vacation in the mountains just to pray and be at peace. In Newark, there was no relief from the pressure. It was very hard for Dan as well. She wanted to get away from all the doctors and all the family that wanted to talk off nothing else but why she should continue the treatment. So Dan rented a lovely cottage in the Adirondack Mountains at Old Forge, NY. He couldn't take all the time off but could come on the weekends. He knew I would be there to take care of Mari-Beth and Emily.

Since it was the end of summer and off season, it was very peaceful. She enjoyed reading, being with Emily and praying and just being at peace. It was a time of really seeking the Lord for her. It was not an easy time for me but we had wonderful times of prayer together. We watched the beginning of the changing of the leaves, enjoyed the scenery, short walks. She loved watching the deer as they wandered fearlessly up to the deck. We went into the village shopping which was great for her because no one knew us. I knew Dan was struggling although he tried not to show it.

I tried to get friends to visit us so we could pray. I didn't know anything about "soaking prayer in those days". I just knew that it seemed the more we prayed over her, the longer we prayed, the better she seemed to feel. I couldn't get anyone but two very close friends to come to pray, Gerry and Ray Deitz. On another day another friend, stopped briefly to say hello. "Where were all the people we prayed with for healing," I thought. There was no real organized ministry but there were people with gifts of prayer but they were all unavailable.

It was Saturday of the second week of our little vacation and we were preparing to leave to return to Newark. Tom and I had gone to early morning Mass at St. Bartholomew's Church in Old Forge. It was September 15, 1984, the Feast of Our Lady of Sorrows. While I was at Mass, I felt the nudge that we should bless Mari-Beth with the Lourdes water I had and pray with her. When we arrived back at the cottage, I asked her if she would like that and she said yes. She was seated in the big lounge chair as I blessed her with the Holy water and began to pray. She blurted out sobbing, "Oh Mom, He didn't give me the answer I wanted". I knelt by the chair and held her in my arms, rocking her and praying in tongues while she sobbed her heart out. It was one of the few times she really cried like she thought all was hopeless. As I was praying, I looked up and saw Dan standing on the stairway with the most unforgettable stricken look on his face. It was one of the most painful moments of my life. I call it "My Pieta". Whenever I see the statue "The Pieta", I remember that day and I marvel at the grace and strength that God gave to sustain me at that very moment. Remembering the seven sorrows of Mary has become a favorite prayer for me.

We started the trip back and on the way Mari-Beth spoke about relenting and taking radiation to try to shrink the tumor. She tried to sound hopeful and optimistic but I knew she was doing this for Dan. Her love for Dan and concern for Dan's anguish and suffering was amazing. She would rather go through the discomfort of treatment than have him suffer the pressure from family and doctors to convince her. She told me later she didn't expect it to work but she had to give in to something because she couldn't stand the pressure from everyone. She said she would tell herself that the radiation rays were the Holy Spirit's rays and pray God would use it somehow.

On the way back, we stopped at my home in Utica, which is at the foothills of the Adirondacks. I called Father Mike and asked him if he could stop to see her and pray with her while we were there. He brought her Holy Communion. As he was about to give the host to her, he first set it on her arm and prayed and then gave it to her. Later he said he felt a nudge from the Lord to do that and in his mind recalled the scripture:

Set me as a seal upon your heart,
as a seal upon your arm.... (Song of Songs 8:6)

God was encouraging Mari-Beth that He was ever present in this whole thing.

IX
Radiation Treatment Begins

I have the strength for everything through him who empowers me.

Philippians 4:13

We arrived back in Newark ready to make new plans for her treatment. Mari-Beth loved giving gifts as well as receiving them. Dan bought her a lovely diamond and emerald ring that brought a smile to her face. He tried to cheer her up. He knew how hard it was for her to make this decision.

We began the many trips to Rochester to the cancer center for the radiation treatments. That was a whole education in itself, especially about people. We always brought Emily with us. Mari-Beth always fussed about dressing her in cute little outfits. She always looked so adorable. Of course, she commanded the attention of everyone wherever we went, to Mari-Beth's delight.

It was interesting to see how Mari-Beth reacted to the different ones who were a part of the team that cared for her. She was definitely a "people person" with a gentle personality and enjoyed most encounters. However, she did not like one of the cancer specialists on the team. She thought he was abrupt and rude when he spoke to her and did not like speaking with him. Each visit for treatment was complete with a chat with the doctors. She dreaded that more than the treatment. During one visit, one of the residents told her she needed to "get a handle on death".

She responded with a smile, saying, *"O' Death, where is thy victory, where is thy sting",* quoting from the scriptures. He just rolled his eyes and shook his head as he walked away. She just smiled and said, "He just doesn't get it!"

We talked about this visit later. She said, "Mom, they think I am in denial and that I don't realize the seriousness of my condition. But I do. I know that I will die without a miracle no matter what treatment I take. We faced that in the beginning and I don't want to have to talk about it every time I go there. I can't believe they don't understand that. They're supposed to be ministering to me not berating me and constantly upsetting me because I don't do what they want. It's my life. They are supposed to be professionals!"

The social worker was no help either. Mari-Beth would not open up to her at all. I questioned her about it. She simply said, "I didn't want to be rude, Mom but she was ridiculous. All she wanted to talk about is dying. Did she really think I was going to open up with that approach? I finally couldn't take it anymore and I said, "Look, I've been on that side of the desk and this just is not working. I'm sorry." And I got up and left. Talk about feeling like you're being social-worked! Whew! I certainly don't need that! I'm sure you never made your clients feel like that."

"I hope not", I said quietly.

However, she always seemed to get along well with most of the nurses. There was one nurse that she loved - Michelle. Michelle always made a fuss over Emily. She was one of the few people Mari-Beth would let hold Emily. Michelle knew how to talk to her and Mari-Beth would open up to her about everything. She was the "real social worker". Mari-Beth looked forward to seeing her. It was a sad day for Mari-Beth if Michelle was off duty. Somehow she made the visits bearable for her. She was a real gift and we thank God for her.

I understood totally. She so wanted people around her to be cheerful and optimistic. She had no illusions about what was happening to her. She just did not want anyone to rob her of the little joy that she had whether she was at home or receiving treatment.

When she first faced her illness, she said to me, "Mom, I want you to make me a promise. No matter what I choose to do, there may come a time when I may just say to the Lord, Jesus, I love you but I can't do this anymore. Take me home. That will be because I'm too tired to fight. You have to promise me that you will not give up even if I do. I want you to keep on believing and praising the Lord even if I die. He can bring me back from the dead if He wants to, you know. Okay? Is it a deal?"

"It's a deal. I promise."

So that was the deal. No one but Dan seemed to understand that we needed to pray and sing and praise the Lord no matter what was going on. That was our strength – the joy of the Lord! It helped to make the days as normal as they could be under the circumstances.

She brought Emily everywhere she went, even to treatment. She was usually very good and it was fun to have her with us. Sometimes we stopped to do some quick shopping on the way home from treatment. There was only one problem. We had to move quickly because Mari-Beth tired so easily. However, when she had her mind set on something, there really was no discussion. So I just rolled with it as well as I could.

One day we stopped to buy shoes for Emily. Emily was scheduled to have her picture taken and Mari-Beth wanted her to have a pair of Mary Janes (little black patent leather slipper-like shoes with a little buckle) for the picture. We put Emily in the stroller and wheeled her through the store not realizing that we were whizzing through crowded aisles of racks of clothing and she began to scream. Poor Emily – Imagine how she felt in that stroller with racks of clothes on every side like she was in a tunnel of every conceivable kind of fabric. We whipped through that store like a cyclone. Mari-Beth had to have those shoes for her. It was that important and I knew better than to argue with her on that issue. Praise the Lord! We got the shoes quickly and got out of the store, lickety split! As soon as we got out side and Emily could see everything, she was fine. Mari-Beth was satisfied that she had the dress and the shoes all set for the photo. Mission accomplished!

Wherever there was a healing Mass Mari-Beth wanted to be there. We attended a healing Mass in Syracuse. Dan's twin brother Tim and his wife Kathy who lived in Syracuse came with us and Mari-Beth was so pleased that they came to Mass. She loved Tim and Kathy and got on well with them. It made her very happy. That night, God relieved the pain in her hip and we noticed she wasn't limping when we came out of church.

It was fall and her cousin Timothy Donovan was getting married in Oswego, NY. They were close cousins and she was very excited about the wedding and wanted to go. I wondered if she could do it. She was adamant, "Mom, after all the time I spent praying that God would find the right girl for Tim, do you really think I am going to miss this?" Dan was in complete agreement.

Of course, that meant a shopping trip for just the appropriate comfortable outfit for her to wear. Most of her clothes were beginning to be pretty loose on her because of the weight loss. She often joked about it saying, "I always wanted to stay in good shape but losing weight this way is not what I had in mind." We found her outfit in a little shop in downtown Newark.

We traveled to Oswego to the wedding. I thought she was so courageous. She looked so happy and pleased with herself that she was able to be there. She had to carry her arm in a sling and on a pillow wherever we went. Her hair was growing in and was only about an inch long and she really looked cute. At the reception, her Aunt Joan said, "I love your hairdo. It's adorable. Only you could wear a hair-do like that." She hadn't noticed her arm. She smiled and said, "It's not really a new hair-do, my hair is just growing in. I have cancer and I lost my hair from the treatment." Poor Aunt Joan! She felt terrible! She had no idea. Not everyone knew at that point. The news hadn't traveled that far. She and Dan even danced at the reception and she looked so contented. I think that was the last time they ever danced. I was so glad we didn't miss that wedding and she was too. In the days to follow, we had lots to share about the wedding and she loved remembering and talking about it.

X
The City of Faith Experience

Again, [amen,] I say to you,
if two of you agree on earth
about anything for which they are to pray,
it shall be granted to them by my heavenly Father.

Matthew 18:19

It was Thanksgiving Day, November 1984 – a time for celebration and thanking God for family. It turned out to be a pretty good day until later that evening. Mari-Beth had gone upstairs to take a bath and discovered more lumps in various places in her body. She was upset because that was blatant evidence that she was getting worse. She was still in the process of receiving radiation treatments at the Rochester Cancer Center. She was very upset that she had agreed to receive the treatment to please everyone else and it was not helping at all.

When she was first diagnosed in May, she told me she wanted to go to the City of Faith at Oral Roberts University in Tulsa, OK, was excited at the prospect and told me that she intended to discuss it with Dan. When I asked her about it a few days later she told me Dan said it was not possible. There was no more discussion about that.

Therefore, I was very surprised when she announced to me they decided to make the trip to Tulsa. I knew she was discouraged at her condition but happy about the trip. She insisted I come with them. I was happy for her because I knew this is what she wanted all along.

There was moment when we were getting ready to leave for Tulsa that was nerve-wracking. She spiked a high temperature.

Since they had told the Cancer Center in Rochester, they were going to Tulsa; they were unable to get any advice from those doctors. Dan and I prayed for wisdom. The Lord told Dan "aspirin or something to reduce the fever". He called the pharmacist who told him the pain medication she was taking had a fever–reducing medication in it so she was covered. We continued with a bath and liquids and continued to prepare for the flight.

She made arrangements for Kelly to care for Emily. Mari-Beth was adamant that no one but Kelly should stay with Emily. So Kelly who is also Emily's Godmother, being the great sister that she is, took time off from her teaching job in NH and flew to Newark to stay with Emily.

Dan, Mari-Beth and I left from the Rochester Airport on November 30th and flew to Tulsa, OK to Oral Roberts University City of Faith Hospital. When we arrived on this incredible campus we could feel the presence of the Lord. A great peace came over me.

The City of Faith Hospital was a magnificent building. More importantly, the atmosphere was peaceful and everywhere we went there was prayer. On admission, she was offered prayer. That was just the beginning of the wonderful prayer

68

experiences on this journey. When she arrived in her room we learned that there were prayer partners on the wards ready to pray whenever one asked.

After all the years I spent in hospitals both as a nurse and as a patient, I could not help but compare and note the difference in current hospitals and centers. "This hospital is amazing," I thought, "this is the way it ought to be."

I trained in a Catholic hospital in the era when there was a kind of hushed aura on the wards. We had Franciscan Sisters who ran the hospital, a priest available for prayer and confession daily and a Chapel with daily Mass available. It always felt like a holy place. This atmosphere reminded me of that awesome peace of being in a holy place, a place where God is welcome.

Since Kim was living in Colorado at the time, she made arrangements to fly in to spend time with us too. It was great to have her there too.

Dan and I had rooms in the hotel that was provided on campus. It was just across the way from the hospital so we were very close to her room. We settled in, not knowing how long we would be there.

One of the first things necessary was blood work. Drawing

blood was not an easy task since Mari-Beth had only one arm available because of the cancer in her right arm, so accessible veins were few and already overworked. The nurse phlebotomist assessed the situation and saw that it didn't look too promising. She gave an optimistic smile and said, "God will help with this". Then she knelt by the bedside poised for the blood draw and said, "Father, you made her and you know where the right vein is so in the Name of Jesus, please show it to me". One puncture and "voila!" she did it. Mari-Beth was very happy. She had weathered some pretty grim experiences previous to this with phlebotomists poking and poking without success.

Mari-Beth was assessed by the oncology team and they recommended a plan of treatment using three aggressive drugs which she had received before in Rochester. She was opposed to taking chemo because of the experience in Rochester and the fact that they told her it wouldn't work anyway. However, she was listening to the Lord and open to what he told her, agreeing with the plan.

The evening before they began the treatment, one of the doctors spent hours with her ministering inner healing for the emotional and spiritual trauma she sustained in the way she had been treated before coming to ORU. He told her that since her spirit appeared to have been truly broken and she needed God to heal that before taking any treatment. Suffice to say, after his time with her, she was well prepared for the treatment. She could not praise this doctor highly enough for the care and compassion he showed her.

The day she was scheduled to start the chemotherapy, I suggested that Dan and Kim take a tour of the campus and I would be happy to stay with Mari-Beth during the treatment. I encouraged them to take in the basketball game at the Mabee Center and the Oral Roberts TV show and go to the prayer tower and they did. Kim was pleased that Sharon Dougherty[1] prayed with her for Mari-Beth.

Her oncology nurse was lovely and very cheerful with a sweet gentle compassionate spirit. She was fairly young and I learned later that she lost a child to cancer and was devoted to this type of nursing. While she administered the chemotherapy, I sat in the room with her and prayed. She very slowly "pushed" the medication IV as opposed to the IV drip Mari-Beth previously received. The room was a holy sanctuary all during the treatment. There was very little conversation and I noticed that her nurse was praying quietly as she ministered the drugs. I was

---

[1] Sharon Daugherty *is a minister in a church with 17,000+ members, author, TV host on the Oral Roberts TV show, missionary, and more...*

sitting in the corner doing the same thing – *praying*. Mari-Beth dozed peacefully through the whole thing.

After the treatment, when she was able to get up and shower with help, she was very pleased that she was only a bit dizzy. She proudly announced that she had only been slightly nauseated since the treatment. I was shocked. She had been given this identical treatment in Rochester and had a violent reaction, vomiting continually. What a gift – she was so soaked in prayer and in the presence of God, she had no violent reaction! I learned that it *IS* possible. God was teaching me how it could be accomplished.

One morning when I came to her room, she seemed excited to tell me something but was having respiratory difficulty and had trouble talking. When we were alone, she motioned to me to give her my journal so she could write something. She wrote with her left hand because her right one was no longer functional. The fact that she that she could learn to write anything with her left hand so quickly and have it be at all legible was amazing to me. She wrote, *"Last night, I heard a woman's voice praying in tongues by my bed and I felt a presence"*. I just smiled and didn't ask anything.

The next day when she was breathing more easily I asked her

about it. I said, "Mari-Beth, tell me about that statement you wrote in my journal". *(Copy of original on the next page)*

She said, "It was in the middle of the night and I was awake. I felt alone and began to feel afraid. I started to reach for the telephone to call your room when *I heard a woman's voice praying in tongues and I felt a presence".* I stopped for a moment and quickly thought – "It's my mother!"

Then she smiled and said, "but it wasn't your voice".

"Who do you think that was?"

"I couldn't see anyone but I felt her presence and I wasn't afraid any more. I believe it was Our Blessed Mother! Do you believe that?"

"Absolutely!"

Copy of the original written by Mari-Beth with her left hand

I keep a copy of this page in my Bible. It's a constant reminder to me of Our Blessed Mother's care and her love for her children.

We asked if Oral Roberts would come and pray with her and were told that he was in Florida at a conference. The next day, there was a knock at the door. When I opened it, I was so surprised. There stood this lovely woman smiling saying, "I'm Evelyn Roberts". I said, "I know, please come in." She proceeded to tell us that Oral was away so she thought she would come instead. She shared some encouraging words with us. She told us the story of the seed that is planted that is so strong that it pushes up through the cement to survive. We felt the power of the Lord in the room. As she prayed with Mari-Beth and with us, "she said, "you have enough of the Holy Spirit here to heal the whole world" and that's exactly how it felt. It was a beautiful visit.

I wrote to Evelyn Roberts after Mari-Beth died and she sent me a lovely note in response.

There were many little encouraging things that were so important. One day when the doctors were making rounds, one of the doctors gave her a scripture to ponder from Malachi about the Lord coming with healing in his wings. The medication bottles from the pharmacy all had scripture on them.

December 6 was the feast of St Nicholas. One of the resident's wives visited us and brought homemade chocolates in honor of the day. Mari-Beth wanted to stay there. She wanted to take one of the nurses home with her because "she always made her feel so safe". Everyone prayed about everything. The whole atmosphere was filled with God's love and healing and peace.

We took a picture of her with her oncologist before we left. She loved him. She thought he was such a gentle and compassionate doctor. She really didn't want to leave. She believed she could heal in that environment. All the staff assured her of their prayer support as they said goodbye.

We arrived there November 30, 1984 and left December 8, 1984. It was a nine day novena although I didn't realize it until we were returning home. It was then that I remembered it was a holy day, the Feast of the Immaculate Conception and we unable to attend Mass because we were "in the air".

We had one "hairy moment" on the plane. Mari-Beth began to experience respiratory distress so I called the flight attendant and asked for oxygen. She told me we needed a prescription for it. Although I explained to her where we had been and that she had cancer that had affected her lungs, she was not moved. As I was beginning to get frustrated and Mari-Beth was struggling to breathe, the Lord arrested me. Suddenly I said, "Never mind, please bring some ice and a towel, we're going to pray". She brought the ice and towel which we put on the back of her neck and I opened my Bible to the Psalms, beginning with Psalm 23. I read loud enough to be heard above the roar of the engine and Dan prayed. I'm sure everyone on the plane heard me as well. I continued until she was breathing more easily.

 As soon as we were on the ground, we had to head to the airport gift shop to pick up a toy for Emily. Mari-Beth was worried Emily would forget her if she was gone too long. Kelly was waiting at home with Emily and a big Welcome Home Banner.

Once we were home, Mari-Beth would return to the cancer center in Rochester with the recommendation from the ORU City of Faith doctors and resume treatment-which she did.

How could it be that she would once again become violently ill here using the same drugs they gave her in Tulsa? Nothing had changed here – same pressures, same negativity. What could anyone do but pray and persevere which we did.

XI
Christmas 1984

The angel said to them,
"Do not be afraid; for behold,
I proclaim to you good news of great joy
that will be for all the people.
For today in the city of David
a savior has been born for you
who is Messiah and Lord."

Luke 2:10,11

It was Christmas and I could see that Mari-Beth was getting weaker all the time. I continued to go to daily Mass. If she was able to go, we would go to the afternoon Mass. We went to prayer meetings when we could. We even went Christmas shopping for Dan's gift. She did her best to write Christmas cards with help. Dan put up the tree. It was Emily's first Christmas and it was special. The joke was that he never put the treetop on. She bugged him about that.

She wanted to spend Christmas in Utica with all the family. Kim and Lee and Joshua were in Colorado and would have to fly here. Mari-Beth insisted they had to come home for Christmas no matter what it took. It didn't look likely but with a lot of prayer and finagling, it was accomplished.

I buzzed round making sure to extend the dining room table to seat thirteen and make it very festive. It was wonderful having them all together including Eleanor Kunkel, Lee's Mom. Later in the afternoon, Gerry and Ray Deitz came to visit and we had a great prayer time. Mari-Beth just loved it. We had no idea that this would be our last Christmas all together but I think she knew. Most of that day for me was a blur, just trying to keep it together for her and be joyful. I just wanted her to enjoy every moment and I think she did.

Christmas time is so special and can be so emotional for me. I cannot help but recall the many years of struggling as a single mom and how God always came through for me. Christmas was always a happy time in our home no matter what life threw in my path and I am extremely grateful.

Once again, God did not leave us disappointed.

XII
1985 - A New Year

And Mary kept all these things,
reflecting on them in her heart.

Luke 2:19

New Year's Day came and went. We hoped things would be looking up for the New Year but there was another problem looming largely on the horizon. Teresa had an ovarian tumor to be removed. She scheduled her surgery for the last week in January so she could recover and return to her job after the February winter break.

The presenting problem was how to take care of both daughters at once in two different locations. Mari-Beth's best friend Mary Grace Tompkins offered to take care of Mari-Beth on her break from school which was wonderful for all of us. There was no one other than me or her sisters she would let help but Mary Grace was the exception. She was like a sister to Mari-Beth. They had a great friendship that developed when they were in college at St. Rose and Mari-Beth was very comfortable with Mary Grace. She and her husband, Dennis were both close to Dan and Mari-Beth. It gave me peace knowing she was there even though it was hard to leave Mari-Beth.

Then Meghan stayed with Mari-Beth for a while during her break from college. That was good for both of them to have time together. We all loved taking care of Emily as well. We all tried to be there for her as she wished.

I returned to Utica to care for Teresa who was confident that God was already taking care of her. After all, hadn't she prayed and asked God for time to let her insurance kick in to cover the surgery and to let her have the surgery during her winter break? Praise be to God! God arrested the growth of the tumor. The tumor that had grown nine times its size in three months had stopped growing. It was as if God halted everything until she could have her surgery. Surely all would be well, I thought. Thank God for her faith and her optimism.

Of course, Mari-Beth tried to encourage Teresa by telling her that she would have a private room, lots of flowers and lots of attention and she would be fine. Interestingly enough, when Teresa was admitted, they said no private rooms were available. I recall talking to Mari-Beth on the hospital phone telling her there were no private rooms for Teresa. She immediately launched into prayer for a private room. I tried to tell her it would be alright but she insisted that Teresa would recover much more quickly in a private room. And lo and behold – a private room opened up just for her! And she did get lots of flowers –eight bouquets – one sent anonymously that she never found out who the sender was. In the following weeks, we brought Mari-Beth to Utica and I took care of all of them for another two weeks.

Teresa was right. They removed an ovary and a fallopian tube with the tumor and she was fine. The fast growing tumor that had grown nine times its original size between the first and second exam had stopped growing in November and was not cancer, thank God!

I recall the day of Teresa's surgery, as I sat in the waiting room trying to pray and stay peaceful. I was actually kind of numb. I held my rosary and had my Bible on my lap. I noticed a gentleman in the corner witnessing to another man and I thought prayerfully, "Dear Lord, I do not want to talk to anyone but you". Sure enough, I was his next project.
As he sat down next to me and started to try to evangelize me, I politely explained that I am Catholic Charismatic, thinking he would know not to continue. Didn't work. He started asking me about the Blessed Virgin Mary and how could I ever believe that she was immaculately conceived and had an immaculate heart? That struck a nerve.

Smiling, I took a deep breath and said, "You know, I look at things very simply. I'm a nurse and I understand fetal circulation. I know that the child in the womb gets its blood supply from the mother's heart through the umbilical cord. I believe The Father in His infinite wisdom, knowing that one drop of the precious blood from His Son's heart was going to be enough to save the whole world would have created the heart that would provide that blood to be nothing less than immaculate. He gave me a blank stare and said, "OH". That ended the conversation. In retrospect, I have to say that the Holy Spirit must have given me that. It was the first time in my life I ever said it, maybe the first time I even thought about it. Teresa recuperated very well. We were very grateful. Mari-Beth missed having me in Newark. Tom was acting strange and wanting me to come home but Mari-Beth was deteriorating slowly and she knew it and begged me not to leave her. I reminded him that I had given my word with his blessing and God had not released me yet.

During the time I had to be in Utica, Mari-Beth had to have a port-a-cath inserted into her chest to facilitate the treatments, eliminating the need to poke her multiple times to find a vein for every treatment. I prayed with her on the phone and tried to encourage her. She called me when she returned home after the procedure and she sounded terrible. I had watched her go through so many painful procedures cheerfully with little or no complaints. She was always so brave, always trying to smile through it all. I could hardly bear it when she explained the pain she endured with this procedure. Sometimes, even now, I can almost hear her say, "Mom, it was so bad, I felt like they stretched me on a rack". To this day, it grieves me deeply when I meditate the crucifixion of our Blessed Lord. I still think of her suffering.

In February, there were healing services being offered at Holy Trinity Church in Utica and she was insistent that she could attend. Teresa was still recuperating but she insisted she could babysit Emily. It was blustery and cold but we went. Things were not going well with Tom but I asked him to help bring her to church and he did. Each thing gave her more and more peace.

On February 7th, I brought her to St. John's Church to meet with Father Mike for confession at her request. I never dreamed it would be her last Confession.

XIII
The Last Days

*"If I die, how will they
ever believe Jesus heals?
Who will tell them?"*
Mari-Beth

Teresa returned to Tupper Lake and resumed her teaching job. I returned to Newark to find Mari-Beth so much weaker than I expected. It was getting harder and harder to keep her spirits buoyed.

During one of those times of discouragement, after a day at the center, she said, "Mom, no matter what happens, I still believe that Jesus can heal me here on earth or take me to heaven. They (referring to her medical caregivers as well as many family and friends) all think I'm crazy now. If I die, how will they ever believe Jesus heals? Who will tell them? My answer was as simple as her question as I responded, without hesitation, "We will, Mari-Beth. Your sisters and I will tell them by the witness of our lives. We can't convince anyone; that's God's job. We can only pray and live our lives the best we can as true believers."

During another one of those times when she became discouraged. She was talking about how badly she felt that there was so much unbelief surrounding her. In tears she said, "They think I am a lunatic because I am always talking about Jesus and His power and what He can do. They really think I'm losing it."

I quickly cut her off and said, "Mari-Beth, listen to me." Suddenly I remembered something I had heard at Bible

Institute and I said, "We can't worry about anyone else. What we have to do is just keep that *LAST DAY* uppermost in our minds. Picture that last day when we are all standing before Him. Picture Jesus, as He looks out over the whole of humanity and says, 'Father, Wait! There is something I want to do. There are brothers and sisters here who proclaimed me before men while they were still on earth. Now I want to recognize them before you.' Then He's going to look into the crowd and see you standing there and say, 'Mari-Beth, come up here to the front. You proclaimed me before all your family and friends and doctors and everyone while you were still on earth. Come on up here. I want to acknowledge you before Our Father. You thought you were last on earth but now you shall be first.'" As I was speaking, I suddenly realized I was actually preaching to her. Imagine?! I watched her face lighten up as she stopped crying and smiled saying, "That's right, for a moment I forgot. Thanks, Mom."

There were many beautiful moments we shared as we went about the daily routine. One day as I helped her dress, she was sitting down and I was standing in front of her. Suddenly she hugged me around my middle and looked up at me like she was about five years old and said, "Mom, thank you for teaching me about Jesus". I treasure that memory.

We had prayer meetings at home all the time. Anyone who visited was welcome to join. Oftentimes, during the day, Mari-Beth and I would sit in the family room in front of the glass sliders and enjoy the view of the beautiful land in back of their home as we sang in "tongues" which she loved to do. She loved to enjoy the "presence of the Lord".

We both had our individual daily prayer time but we always shared our thoughts and prayed together every day. She and Dan had their own private prayer time together as well. She was always interested to hear what I was hearing from the Lord each day and would tell me what God was saying to her each day.

She loved people but was very selective about who she allowed to visit because she had keen sense of the Spirit and gift of discernment. She had learned to guard her peace and I respected that as she wished.

She wanted a happy atmosphere and did her best to achieve that. She was very cheerful especially around Emily. She just loved to watch her. She was so proud of her. She would say very often to me, "Emily will always be very special to you, won't she, Mom?" I would just smile because she knew that was true. In retrospect, it seems that maybe she was reassuring herself for a time when she would not be around. I think she was trying to secure that closeness for Emily and me.

I always went to the Cancer Center with her and Dan. On one particular day I felt like I needed to stay home. When she arrived home, she was in tears as she brushed by me, going up to her room, angrily whispering, "They changed the treatment!". That's all she would say but many tears were shed in quiet.

She continued to deteriorate. One day she became so weak, we took her to the hospital in Rochester. The doctor examined her and wanted to discharge her but when she started to get up, she was so weak she almost collapsed. She whispered to me, "They think I'm dying, that's why they don't want to admit me." Dan insisted they admit her.

We had to wait for a room. As we were walking down the hospital corridor, I was praying, "Lord, I missed my daily Mass this morning. How I wish I could go to Mass." Suddenly I heard coming from the loud speaker, "there will be Catholic Mass in the chapel at noon". It was almost noon. I was thrilled. It was the last thing I expected since this was not a Catholic hospital. So we went to Mass. During the prayer of the faithful, I prayed aloud for peace as we awaited the Lord.

Mari-Beth was admitted and I went down to find out where the Catholic chaplain might be. I was told to wait in the lobby. As I sat there alone with the Lord and my thoughts, I was feeling kind of numb. A woman approached me saying, "I was at noon Mass and I saw you with your daughter and was so moved by your prayer and you seem so peaceful." We chatted for a few moments and she said she would pray for us. I have no idea who she was but I felt blessed.

I saw the chaplain and asked him if he would visit Mari-Beth. I explained her situation and he assured me he would. I returned to her room to wait.

When he arrived Mari-Beth was dozing so he sat by the bedside for awhile, not wanting to disturb her. When she began to stir a bit, he introduced himself quietly and said, "I understand you are having a difficult time, Mari-Beth."

Her eyes opened wide and she said, "God says in his Word, "if you keep my commandments and walk in my ways, I will give you long life and length of days" and closed her eyes. Father looked at me and I laughed and said, "It seems she has a new gift – holy boldness".
At that, she opened her eyes again and said, "And I remind Him daily!" We all laughed.

He spent time with her ministering to her as best he could, not really knowing her, and we were grateful.

They needed to draw blood and they couldn't use the port-a-cath and were contemplating a site, in whispers saying femoral, perhaps. The doctors tried to get me to leave the room and Mari-Beth gave me that look that said, "Don't leave me."
 I just smiled at the team and said, "You don't understand. I don't need to leave. I'm a nurse and I will be fine and trust me, you'll be glad I stayed." Then I turned and said to Mari-Beth, "Just look at me and pay no attention to what they are doing. Here's what we're going to do. Together you and I are going to say, over and over until they're finished. *JESUS! JESUS! JESUS!* And God is going to take care of everything." We did and God did. The doctors said nothing but they never asked me to leave again.

It was such a difficult time. They did what they could for her during that brief hospital stay to strengthen her to go home. But the outlook was bleak.

Meghan was at Niagara University which was too far to come to visit very often. She called and told me she was spending the weekend in Corning, NH with a roommate. I had a hard time telling her to come to the hospital in Rochester without telling her the time was short. I was very curt with her on the phone. She got the message and decided to come to the hospital. All I can remember is that she had a ridiculous black outfit on, obviously borrowed from her friends. When she walked in, Mari-Beth said, "Meghan, really? – black?"

Meghan, looking bewildered, responded, "What? You don't like my outfit?"

"I'm not dead yet".

"Sorry." And they both laughed.

I always trusted that the Lord would prepare me when and if the time came and He is faithful. As Dan and I were by her bedside one day, listening to the discharge plans from the team, I had a clear revelation. I had a mental vision of our Lord dying on the cross with John and our blessed Mother standing at the foot of the cross and I heard the words, "It is finished". Suddenly, I had a flash of remembrance of a word in my journal that I had read to Mari-Beth the day before that referred to Dan as my son. Mari-Beth remarked about that. She said, "That's nice, Mom, that's the first time I ever heard God refer to Dan as your son." I agreed but didn't understand it until that moment.

In the days to follow, I would realize that no matter what happened God would expect me to pray for Dan as a spiritual son forever. As Mary as my example, I would be faithful to that word and forever grateful.

We all gathered with the doctors and the team around her bed to make plans for her discharge. It was so very difficult to realize the end was near. They wanted to give her morphine to go home on and she did not want it. She looked at me with that sad pleading look and said to me, "Mom, you know how I feel about taking morphine." (She had a hard time about some of the drugs, always wanting to be alert enough to praise the Lord).

"I know, Mari-Beth, but it is a good drug and will help your breathing."

She gave me that sad look of acquiescence and said, "alright, if I have to".

Then suddenly she looked around and said, "Where's Kelly? Kelly, where are you?" She was behind the curtain, crying. Mari-Beth said, "What are you doing? Come here." She came to the bedside and they hugged, with Kelly crying and Mari-Beth saying, "Come on, Kel, don't be so dopey." That was a beautiful moment no matter how sad.

Peter and Kelly were there and knew that I had to make more arrangements and the time was short. I told them I needed to return to Utica for the day. I had things to attend to. I told Mari-Beth I needed to get my hair done and pick up some more linens and things, including my favorite blue vase for the beautiful roses Peter had brought her. She refused to be discharged until I returned so I made haste to return as quickly as I could. It was a lot of driving for one day.

When I returned, their friend Father Ken Doyle was there preparing to celebrate Mass at her bedside. With him was another of their friends and Father jokingly said, "We have a Jewish altar boy." Mari-Beth asked some of the staff to join. She especially wanted the young resident Mike there. He had been so kind to her and brought her a Michael Talbot tape to listen to.

Mass was beautiful. Father asked Mari-Beth if she had a favorite song she would like us to sing after Communion. She smilingly answered, "Be Not Afraid". As we sang, she looked at Dan and saw that he was crying. She reached out to him saying, "Oh, I'm so sorry, I forgot you're so sentimental." She explained that it was one of the songs from their wedding Mass. That seemed to lift the mood as she could always seem to do.

Naturally, this was very hard on Dan. One day we had a

birthday cake for him while she was in the hospital. I almost forgot and wanted to light the candles until Mari-Beth arrested me. "Mom, did you forget? I have oxygen. Do you want to blow us all up?" That really put a new spin on the conversation. They loved it. We treasured any little spark of joy we could resurrect. It was indeed our strength.

As we were leaving, one of her favorite nurses, Karen, stopped in the corridor to say goodbye. Mari-Beth wanted to have a prayer with Karen because she was so grateful that she helped her with her breathing exercises that made her calm down many times.

There were so many times Mari-Beth wanted to pray with someone or for someone or give them a finger rosary to encourage them. She always had her rosary or finger rosary with her at all times. One time, while in the hospital, I thought she was asleep with her rosary in her hand when she opened her eyes and said, "Mom, I was just praying for Mary G. Her pain is so great. Would you send her some white rosebuds with a blue ribbon (for Our Blessed Mother) to let her know we are praying for her?" Mary G. was a woman who was terminally ill with cancer back in Utica.

On the day of her discharge from the hospital, we were making arrangements to leave. I had driven my little own red Cavalier to the hospital. We had traveled so many hours in this car. She helped me buy it and it was special. She liked it so much Dan bought her a little red car and told her it would be there when she was ready to drive. Dan also had driven his car and I was sure she would drive home with him. But she was insistent that she would drive home with me in my little red car. I wasn't terribly comfortable with that. It was an hour long drive and she had an oxygen tank to bring with her as well. Dan and I looked at each other and shrugged our shoulders as if to say, "Whatever you want is fine with us." So she climbed into the front seat of my car with me, oxygen tank and all. The ride was very peaceful all the way to Newark and she seemed contented. We listened to our Christian music and prayed.

As we entered their home, she insisted on checking the kitchen before going to her room, to see if Dan had the new dishwasher installed while she was gone. She was concerned about me having too many dishes to wash.

While she was in the hospital, Dan bought a waterbed for them. Filling the waterbed with the hose would make a good comedy but it's not one of my favorite memories. Accomplishing the task was the important thing. She already had problems with her skin integrity and it was sorely needed to try to make her as comfortable as possible.

She settled in with a morphine pump to relieve her pain. Dan hired a nurse aid to help with her daily care. Family came by to visit, knowing it would probably be the last. She was particular about who she would see and we tried to abide by her wishes.

Eileen Donovan, a close cousin came to visit her. The thing she was most concerned about was that she didn't want to upset Eileen by the way she looked. She said, "Mom, I really don't want to scare her." We both laughed and I assured her that it would be fine.

My sister Eileen brought Gram Lavery, my mother, to visit. That was hard for my Mom but Gram was so peaceful with Mari-Beth and Mari-Beth was so happy to see her. "Mom, it was so great to see Gram. She gave me this little medal (Divine Mercy Medal) and told me not to be afraid, just to keep saying, "Jesus, I trust in you".

I was sorry for my mom to be facing the loss of another grandchild. She later lamented to me, saying, "It doesn't make any sense to me. It doesn't seem right. She's so young." My mom grappled with the thought of grandchildren dying before their grandparents.

XIV
Her Last Day

Jesus told her, "I am the resurrection and the life;
whoever believes in me, even if he dies, will live,
and everyone who lives and believes in me
will never die..."

John 11:25,26a

There was so much to do every day, it helped me stay strong. I was grateful for that. I had my time with the Lord every morning early, attended 6:00 AM Mass and time with the Lord before I retired. He truly walked with me through every day.

Mari-Beth had shared with me a dream that she died. I asked her if she was afraid. She said, "Yes."

I replied in a firm voice, "Well, if that was God, then you take that right back to Him and ask Him about that. He promised that He would be with us and there would be no fear." She never mentioned it again so I have to believe He gave her a peace about it.

The night before she died, I helped her out of bed to use the bedside commode (she was still that independent, insisting to get up with help). Then I spent a few moments talking with her. She said, "Mom, last night I did not have a peaceful night's sleep, I hope tonight will be better." I prayed over her and assured her that she would sleep peacefully. We said, "I love you" to each other and goodnight. Mari-Beth was greatly comforted that Dan slept alongside her.

Morning came and I began my time in prayer. The Lord told me not to go to Mass but to take care of myself and not go into

Mari-Beth's room until He told me to. I prayed, showered, dressed, and had a quick breakfast. Emily was still asleep.

About 7:00 AM, the Lord said, "Now you may go in". It was so still in the room. Dan woke up and was unable to rouse Mari-Beth. It appeared that she had slipped into a coma. We wondered if it was the morphine. Dan phoned the doctor and he said to stop the drip altogether and wait to see if she rallied. If not, we would know that she was in a coma. She didn't wake up.

We tried to keep the room as normal and peaceful as possible with her Christian Music playing the way she loved it. When Emily was awake, she played in her playpen in the corner of the room.

Dan invited three of his friends from church to come and pray at the bedside. Father Doyle had called Father Ralph DiOrio who has a healing ministry. Father DiOrio called and Dan put the phone to Mari-Beth's ear as Father prayed with her over the phone.

I spent most of my time, kneeling by the bedside, praying my rosary, as did Dan's mother. I talked to Mari-Beth as well but mostly we just prayed and watched and waited.

I wondered if Mari-Beth could hear me as I spoke to her and then I *saw one tear trickle down her cheek from her left eye* and I knew. Suddenly, a memory came rushing into my mind. It happened several years before any of this began. In my daily routine as a social worker, my friend, Elizabeth and I used our morning break to go across the street from the office to an Anglican Church that had a chapel to Our Blessed Mother that was open for prayer during the day. We had just enough time to run cross the street, pray for a few minutes and be back to work on time. I was learning to listen to hear the voice of the Lord and that's what I did. For several days, I would feel so sad but would *shed only one tear from my left eye* and I didn't understand it. Then one day I thought I heard the Lord ask me if I knew that my girls all belonged to Him and I said I did. Then He impressed me of a suffering to come involving them, I thought just one of them, which I did not understand and I did not want to hear. I wasn't exactly sure of what I heard but eventually I felt like I had to share it with someone (and of course I hoped I was wrong). So I shared it with Elizabeth and then I let it go. But I prayed very hard for them every day. Now I understood. The tear was the confirmation after all these years.

The day wore on and she didn't wake up. I had been with her for a long time not wanting to leave her side. Dan and Tom and Dan's mother were there and convinced me to go downstairs and take a break. I poured a cup of tea and opened my Bible to a Psalm God directed me to read:

> *"I will listen for what God, the LORD, has to say;*
> *surely he will speak of peace*
> *To his people and to his faithful."*. *Psalm 85:9*

I looked at the footnote and it said, *"The prophet listens to God's revelation"*.

Just then, they called me back upstairs. She had stopped breathing. Dan had to make the hard decision to call for the rescue team to try to resuscitate. He looked at and me and I said, "You're right, it's what she wanted. She said to do whatever it takes". Meanwhile, I continued to call to her and to call out to the Lord. I remember praying Psalm 23 because I believed she could still hear. Interestingly enough, that was the first time I ever recited it. I wasn't even aware that I had it in my memory. As they tried to resuscitate her, all I could say was JESUS, JESUS, JESUS, over and over again.

As they put her in the ambulance, they wouldn't let me or Dan go in the ambulance. We followed them to the Newark hospital where she was pronounced dead.

We were allowed to go in to see her as she lay in the emergency room waiting for the undertaker. As they said goodbye and left,

I wanted to remain with her a bit longer. The ER nurse wanted me to leave but I prevailed upon her to allow me to stay. She was doubtful. I said to her, "I am not going to faint or anything else. I just want to talk to her for a few minutes".

Mari-Beth looked so beautiful, this child that I brought into the world, so dearly loved by everyone. Now I had to give her back. She was at peace for the first time in months. All I could do was tell her how much I loved her and how proud I was to be her mother. I told her I did my best and I hoped she knew I tried to do everything I knew to do. Even now, I can picture that moment and her beautiful, peaceful face.

When I left her, I rode the elevator with everyone else just looking at me. No one said a word. I said nothing.

When I got in the car with Tom, the dam broke and I sobbed like never before nor have I since. It lasted all the way back to Dan's. When I got in the house, I could hear myself sobbing, "My little girl is gone." Everyone was hugging and crying. What could be worse than this?

When I calmed down, I realized we should prepare her clothes to take to the undertaker. She would need long sleeves to cover the affected arm. She only had one long-sleeved dressy dress, a bluish, filmy crepe that needed a camisole underneath. Of course, I would give her one of mine. The family joke is that even in death, she took some of my lingerie. Living with all girls, nothing was sacred. Everyone shared just about everything.

We managed to get through the wake, sharing with friends and family. One great thing about a family is that somehow sharing the grief seems to give you the strength to get through it all.

XV
Saying Goodbye

Yes, in joy you shall go forth,
in peace you shall be brought home;
Mountains and hills shall break out in song before you,
all trees of the field shall clap their hands.

Isaiah 55:12

W e prepared for the funeral, each one of us deciding not to wear black as Mari-Beth would have wanted it.

The morning of the funeral, Kelly came to me and said, "Mom, you'll never guess what reading the Lord gave me to meditate during my prayer time; the reading about Martha and Mary and how Mary chose the better portion.

"Of course," she laughed, "she did it again. She chose the better portion and left me with the mess to clean up." Kelly and Mari-Beth shared a very close bond as sisters. They always joked about growing old and being "two little old raisins together". I knew this was extremely difficult for her.

I smiled and hugged her, thinking, "how beautiful it is that even in her grief, Kelly was listening to the Lord". God is good.

We arrived at St. Michael's Church for the funeral; I spotted an aunt and uncle who had made a special effort to be there. I broke from the procession to hug them both. As I entered the church, I saw a priest on the altar with Father Doyle. I could hardly believe it. My spiritual director, Father Mike Bassano had travelled from Utica to be here and I hadn't even asked. But, oh, how I needed to see him there. He heard the Lord tell him to come. Another blessing from the Lord!

Teresa had chosen a bright red dress to wear and did one of the readings at Mass. Father Doyle spoke beautifully of Mari-Beth. We sang her favorite, "Be Not Afraid", allowing us all to cry some more. After communion, he invited the congregation to spontaneous prayer and praise saying, "this is the way Mari-Beth loved to pray". Many of us prayed in "tongues" and it was beautiful and healing. I heard a voice behind us say in a loud whisper, "WHAT! Was that?"

I sighed and thought, "you poor thing, after all this time and all her witnessing and suffering, you still don't get it."

The recessional was "On Eagles Wings", just as she would have it. Sharing back at their house was noisy and confusing and I just kept in motion to keep my peace.

The days that followed were difficult. We drove to Oswego to see my Mom with Emily one day. When we returned, Dan was wrapped in Mari-Beth's comforter on the sofa, so unlike him but we were all looking for comfort.

Kim offered to stay to help with Emily for a couple of weeks so Dan could get his bearings. I began to prepare to leave when Dan told us he was invited to make a Cursillo weekend with some people from his parish. I told him I would be glad to stay the weekend with Kim, Josh and Emily if it would help. So I did. I was concerned about Kim as well. She just found out she

109

was pregnant. (Another prayer of Mari-Beth's was answered.) I stayed until Sunday night when Dan returned. As I drove back to Utica I cried all the way, knowing that would be the last time I'd stay at Dan's house.

My job here was done but the journey was not really over – it simply moved into the next place – the loss, the grief, the suffering that would eventually bring healing.

Photo of her gravestone

No one has ever seen God. But, if we love one another,
God lives in union with us, and his love is made perfect in us.
1 John 4:12 (Good News Bible)
(Scripture quote on the gravestone)

XVI
Life Goes On

My child, when you come to serve the Lord,
prepare yourself for trials.

Sirach 2:1

My return home to resume my life was full of more disasters just waiting to happen. In the months to follow, I would experience Tom's unfaithfulness and the loss of our marriage, many friends, my church group and be subjected to more trials at work. The pastor had disbanded the prayer group. I was verbally ousted by a parishioner while the pastor watched in the background for reasons still unknown to me.

As each thing happened to me, I just got quieter and quieter. I had no inclination to fight for anything. I made some half-hearted moves in an effort to survive but I accepted it all. I'd been through the pain of rejection and divorce before. I knew I couldn't change anyone but myself so I just *tied a bigger knot in my rope and tried to hold on*, so to speak.

While I was still a parishioner in this parish, I went to the prayer meeting. I heard this woman's husband had cancer and I thought I should pray for him. All I did was participate in the prayer meeting along with everyone else. After the prayer meeting, his wife accosted me telling to leave the parish and find someplace else to pray, that I was not welcome. I was so vulnerable and hurt; I just burst into tears, sobbing as I looked up and saw the pastor peeking through the door that was ajar. He was watching the whole thing and never did a thing. When she was finished and saw what she had done, she thought maybe we could be friends. I simply said, "I don't think so." I prayed a Hail Mary with her and departed. I never went back.

I wanted to return to work but I had to wait until my leave was over, they told me. When I did return, it was no picnic. I had tendonitis in both wrists and writing applications was very painful. So I went to my supervisor who was also a friend of mine, I thought, and asked to be relieved of this part till I was out of pain. Her response was a terse, "you'll handle it, Sarah, you always do." So much for compassion, I thought.

"Had the whole world gone mad?" I thought. If God was stripping everything away, I guess I'd just have to let him. How is it that people actually believe that God leaves us when someone dies or our prayer isn't answered the way we expected? It was difficult to be so abandoned by everyone but a faithful few. But as my friend and prayer partner Gerry always said, "When they all go out, there is always Jesus who never leaves.' Thank you, Lord!

Oh, how I longed for someone to praise the Lord with. I didn't need sympathy and I certainly wasn't going to receive understanding. Everyone seemed to have their own agenda. My best prayer partners were my daughters and they were all scattered. Kimberly in Colorado, Kelly in NH, Teresa in the Adirondack Mts., Meghan at Niagara University and of course, Mari-Beth, now in eternity.

One morning after Mass, as I talked with the Lord, I complained about this. Then I heard Him say, "Go where they are".
"Who Lord?" I asked.
"Go where they are praising my name"
I immediately thought of a group called "The Alleluia Group". I thought they used to meet on Tuesdays at 10AM at a church in East Utica. I had never been to that group but I didn't care. I looked at the clock and saw that it was just 9:30. I grabbed my coat and off I went.

There they were, praising the Lord in a prayer meeting and happy to greet me. During the prayer meeting, I uttered a prophecy that was confirmed. I didn't notice until the meeting was over that there was a priest in the group. I heard the Lord nudge me to approach him.

I introduced myself to him and said, "Where does one go to serve the Lord and grow in the gift of prophecy?" He smiled and said, "You have come to the right person." He was not only an associate of that parish but also the regional liaison for the Charismatic Renewal in our diocese.

That was the beginning of a time of being able to resume the use of the gift of prophecy under his guidance. He asked me to gather others who were being used in the gift of prophecy into a group which I did. We met for prayer monthly to listen to the Lord and pray for each other. We attended the monthly Charismatic Masses wherever they were held in our region and served as the prophetic group at the Mass. It was a time of quiet joy in the midst of my time of grief. I love the Holy Mass and I treasured this opportunity to serve.

There was the ever present dark cloud of this other priest hanging over my head but I totally submitted to the church. I couldn't figure out what I did or what he thought I did. Still I obeyed when I was told by the Charismatic regional liaison to write a letter of apology to this priest and ask to meet with him. I did exactly as I was told. He never responded.

I went to a conference and went to confession to a priest who was in a position of authority in our diocese. I brought my dilemma to confession. He told me to forget about it and find another parish to attend which I did.

One Saturday, I heard of a special workshop being held in

another church so I decided to attend. As I walked in, not one person welcomed me and I knew many of them pretty well. It grew silent in the room until this very kind priest who was pastor greeted me with a big smile saying, "You are always welcome in my church." As time went on, a few made friendly gestures but it was never the same. I guess they thought God had left me but oh how wrong they were.

For each step I took, I would seek the Lord, pray with my spiritual director and hope for the best. Being who I am, although I understood *whose* I am, I continued to wonder. With my failed marriage, my daughter's death, the rejection of the pastor and the silence of those I thought were my friends, I couldn't have felt more abandoned. However, the Lord had not abandoned me and He continually reminded of that.

Early in my spiritual growth, God gave me an exhortation in prayer. He said, *"If you are obedient and stay in the church, I will always provide for you a holy priest that will be your saving grace."* (At that time many were leaving the Catholic Church for other denominations). God is faithful. He has never let me down.

Time passed painfully slow during these days when I was so alone. I would spend my grieving time praying and writing my thoughts, some poetry and just trying to live one day at a time.

On one of these dark days, as I arrived home from work and checked the mail, I got a surprise in a letter. The letter was from a woman I met briefly at a Steubenville Bible Institute conference the previous summer. She enclosed a prophecy I had given at the conference with her letter. She said the Lord nudged her to write to encourage me which she truly accomplished. It also reminded me of Mari-Beth's favorite song, "In a Little While" by Amy Grant. It really lifted me up as well as allowed me to have a "*good cry*"

My children tried to encourage me from afar. Sometimes I visited Kelly and Peter Dunn in New Hampshire which was always healing for me. They belonged to a prayer group so I went to the prayer meeting with them. Kelly was studying for her Masters Degree in Special Education at Notre Dame College in Manchester. During one of my visits she was leading the students at graduation and invited me to attend. It was most enjoyable since Erma Bombeck, a favorite author of mine, was the guest speaker.

These were just times to be with family and walk through the pain. Some days were difficult and some were "just days". I knew God was with me and I just kept going to work each day, going to daily Mass and praising the Lord, not asking anything in particular. I just wanted to hear his voice and know I was doing His will.

The tendonitis in both wrists was painful but I believed He
would take care of it. When there was no improvement after
much prayer, I made an appointment with a specialist, a hand
surgeon. After examination, he confirmed tendonitis in both
wrists that was more severe in the right wrist. He gave me
choices to consider; cortisone injections, surgery or live with
the pain that would probably get worse. I witnessed my faith to
him, told him I would pray about it and if God told me to
come back to be treated, I would be back.

Months later, I attended a charismatic conference at Notre
Dame University in South Bend, Indiana with Meghan, Kelly
and Peter. During a praise session led by John Wimber, a well
known Pentecostal preacher, I experienced the healing touch of
God. I had both arms raised in the air, praising the Lord and I
suddenly realized I had no pain in my wrists. I twisted my
wrists every which way and there was absolutely no pain! I was
ecstatic - no pain for the first time in months. God healed me
instantly and completely and I wasn't even asking at that
moment. There was no one laying hands on me for healing. I
wasn't even thinking about healing. I was simply praising the
Lord and He reached down and healed me!

How great is our God? In the middle of the worse time in my life, He healed my wrists completely with one touch, ever reminding me that He is always with me, no matter what it looks like. That was May 1986. Praise the Lord!

XVII
An Unexpected Pilgrimage

You are witnesses of these things.
And [behold] I am sending
the promise of my Father upon you;
but stay in the city until you are
clothed with power from on high."

Luke 24: 48,49

As our prophetic group continued to serve in the Charismatic Mass, we were asked to help organize and serve a special celebration in honor of Our Lady and the seventh anniversary of the reported apparitions in Medjugorje, Yugoslavia. I was doing much of the work in preparation and organizing it.

One morning during my prayer time, as I wrote the word I heard from the Lord, I heard that I would be going to Medjugorje. When I finished writing, I laughed to myself, "Wow, you're so involved in this celebration, now you think you are going there." I laughed about it as I drove to work.

At work, I had a bit of a mishap. I tripped going to the copy machine, fell and bumped my head. So embarrassed that someone might have seen me fall, I got up quickly and nervously rushed back to my desk. Unfortunately, I had to report it and go to the doctor to be checked out.

As I was going into the doctor's office I met my friend, Liz. I told her, "I just don't have time for this." So she prayed with me. The doctor said the usual, "watch for any symptoms, take it easy, here is a prescription for pain. Looks like you are alright. Go home and rest".

Driving home, I decided to go to the printers to order the

posters for the Mass, saying to myself, "nothing is going to stop this Mass and if this is an attack from the enemy, I'll go one better. Just for that, I'll add Our Lady of Medjugorje's picture to the poster to glorify God all the more."

Just as I arrived home, the phone rang. It was my friend, Gerry. She said, "I felt the Lord nudging me to call you and tell you this. I am going on pilgrimage to Medjugorje for the 7th Anniversary of the reported apparitions of Our Lady. There are still two vacancies in the group. I believe God wants you to go."

I scoffed at the suggestion, "thank you for the thought. However, I have neither the time, the money nor the desire to fly over the ocean."
She concluded, "Well, just pray about it anyway."

I called my daughter Teresa for prayer for my injury. I had no intention of filling the prescription. I wanted to make sure I would be okay to return to work in the morning. In speaking to her, I related the details of the day as well. Teresa said, "Mom, maybe the Lord allowed this to get your attention. Maybe you should pray about going to Medjugorje."
"Really?"
She prayed for me and when I got off the phone, I took it to

the Lord.

Amazingly, within two weeks, I had secured the time off from my job, the reservation, my passport and visa and the money. I was able to delegate everything to be covered for the special Mass and assured Father that all would be taken care of. Our generous God always puts things in place for us once we take the first step. Oh how He blesses us!

I didn't realize the significance of this pilgrimage at the time. The opportunity to be in the place of the apparitions of Our Blessed Mother Mary in our times in itself was overwhelming. The breathtaking experience of seeing the "miracle of the sun" four times was indescribable. Talking with the visionaries, meeting people from other countries, climbing Mt Krezivac (where I made my consecration to the Sacred Heart of Jesus and the Immaculate Heart of Mary with my friend Betty and a seminarian named Andrew). Going to Confession in the field well as three of the rosaries I brought turned gold are only a few of the memories I hold. Most importantly of all, was the gift of peace I received that is with me even to this day. Thank God for our Lady of Medjugorje, Queen of Peace!

I was so moved by this trip that when the opportunity presented itself in 1989 to return the following year, I went again. I was there to experience Divine Mercy Sunday that was indescribably beautiful and powerful for me. I knew God was healing me and preparing me to move on. Somehow I knew I was ready to do whatever He asked and I was once again overwhelmed with a great peace.

God carried me for those four years, and then again gave me a nudge to move to New Hampshire where most of my family now lived. I had been hearing the Lord say I would move to New Hampshire for well over four years, actually before I married Tom. It didn't make sense then because Mari-Beth was in Newark, NY and Kimberly in Colorado and Kelly was in New Hampshire. Teresa and Meghan were still in college. I thought I wasn't hearing clearly. As the years passed, I learned that God often tells me things long before the propitious time, even years.

I began to pray about it seriously. Here I was, pretty much alone. My job and the small prophetic community were about the extent of my socialization. My daily Mass as always was my salvation. I considered what would be involved in taking early retirement from Social Services as well. Relocating without finding a job first was out of the question.

On one of my visits to New Hampshire, I decided to give the

job search serious effort. At that time, in my job at Social Services, I worked in the employment unit. That was one of the thirteen placements I enjoyed in twenty three years. Some were promotions and some were lateral transfers. All were blessings of great experience. We tried to help welfare recipients in every way back to employment and self-sufficiency. I thought to myself, "Here is a chance to do what you advocate every day."

I decided to take one day and "hit the pavement" to job search. I took the daily newspaper and circled seven possible job openings for social worker. With my resume in hand, I set out for the day. My daughter, Kelly was kind enough to drive me around the city to save time. I actually got three interviews "on the spot" and one job offer to consider.

The job was in a nursing home. I told the interviewer that I needed to work out some details regarding the lease on my apartment before I could say yes. I figured that if this was really God's plan, all would fall into place. Much to my surprise, I was unable to break the lease on my apartment. I could arrange a sublet or pay till the lease was up, an amount that was prohibitive. So that was the end of that, I thought.

About a year and a half later, I had the nudge again. I wasn't about to step out and go through the same thing. I continued to hear that word. I was visiting and my daughter and son-in-law took me to their prayer meeting. Secretly, I put a petition in the prayer basket saying, "Lord, if you want me in New Hampshire, show me a door and open it".

After the prayer meeting was over, a woman came up to me and said, "I believe I have a word from the Lord for you but I don't think you want to hear it".
I was skeptical but I smiled and said, "Okay".
 She said, "God told me to tell you that there is an opening for an RN on the night shift at the nursing home where I work." She was right. I didn't want to hear it. To take that job meant that I would go back to nursing which I hadn't done it twenty three years. Although my New York license was current, I would probably have to take a refresher course to get my license in New Hampshire. I thanked her and told her I would pray about it.

This was in July and I was on vacation, staying with my family. I shared it with them. They prayed with me and we discerned I should check it out. Interestingly enough, the job was at the same nursing home that offered me the social workers position a year and a half previous to this time.

I called and was interviewed and offered the job. Although a refresher course was required, I would be able to work as an assistant until I passed the refresher course and the administration would even pay for the course. I found a condo that was a possibility. When I asked the Lord about a date, He told me September. It just so happened that my lease was up September 1st. Everything fell into place within two weeks and I made arrangements to move.

There was one very painful thing I had to do before I could leave besides saying goodbye to friends and colleagues. My eldest sister Kathleen had been in a coma post neurosurgery in a Syracuse, NY hospital since October.

 She was the eldest of our family of nine children and we were close. She was a remarkable woman who raised four children and weathered a divorce after her first brain tumor surgery. She suffered more pain and rejection in the following almost twenty years than I can describe but never lost her faith or her kindness to others. She always had a smile no matter what. The tumor grew again and she had surgery which left her in a coma. Before her surgery, we prayed. She said."I would like God to heal me but if I am not going to be good for anything I don't want Him to leave me here. He can take me home." I knew it would be painful for me to give up those visits, always praying and hoping she would wake up. I went to visit her and even in her coma I think she understood what I was doing. I somehow knew that was my final goodbye. She died the following June 23, 1990.

XVIII
On to New Hampshire

See, I am sending an angel before you,
to guard you on the way
and bring you to the place I have prepared.

Exodus 23:20

September 1, 1989, we loaded my little U Haul trailer and left Utica bound for Manchester, NH. Since I had gotten rid of most of my belongings, save the necessities, the trailer provided ample space for my things. My family helped in every way which really made all the difference. Making a move like this totally alone would have been a nightmare, if possible at all.

 It was both exhilarating and frightening all at the same time. What was I thinking? At my age, I was starting all over, in a strange city, in a new job, in new living arrangements, in a new church and no friends. "Can I really do this at age 55?" I asked myself.   I knew it was now or never. I joked with my family that I had them nearby and had the essentials all in place, especially my church and my hairdresser. I had prayed and the Lord showed me enough signs to know it was right. I knew God was with me. So with my ever-present guardian angel, Eva, and the help of my family, I made the move and never really looked back.

Let me tell you about my angel Eva. I always knew I had a guardian angel who is always with me. My Mother taught me to pray to my guardian angel for help. I never knew anything about learning your angel's name or naming your angel. In some of the prayer groups, there was discussion about the importance of angels and learning their names. A kind gentleman in one of the prayer groups offered me a cassette tape of a teaching he had shared in the group about angels. I was reluctant but appreciated his kindness and took the tape, left it in my car and forgot it for awhile.

One day driving home, I thought of it and put it in the tape deck. It was full of scripture references and as I drove along listening to the teaching I heard, "your *angel's name is* EVA". I stopped the tape and prayed. I thought, "Eva is not a familiar name to me: no one I know has that name, no Evas in our family." Then I recalled a teaching I heard a while back about the true AVE of Mary. Eve was the disobedient woman in the beginning. Mary was the obedient woman who turned everything around for humanity. She was Available, Vulnerable and Expectant. I pray a lot about being obedient to the Word. It made sense.

As soon as I got home, I called the priest who was our director of the prophetic ministry. and told him about it. He confirmed that teaching about Mary. So from that day on, I called my angel by name, Eva.

One of the first things I wanted to do was to find a parish. My children attended St. Catherine of Siena which was closer to their home but I went to a prayer meeting at Ste. Marie Parish community on the west side of Manchester. I decided to go to Confession there. I had always found spiritual direction in the Sacrament of Confession so I was sure this was the first step. Wouldn't you know there would be obstacles to my getting there? It took me two weeks to return to Sainte Marie Parish and even then there was a problem. There was a Riverfest celebration going on causing traffic jams and detours. Being unfamiliar with the area didn't help any. By the time I got to the church, it was ten past four. I was sure I was too late because Mass started at four. The Lord prompted to go in anyway. Lo and behold, there was a priest in the confessional sitting there like he was waiting for me. He said, "Come right in". I made my confession and later as I knelt to pray my penance I heard "ask him for spiritual direction".

When I arrived back at my daughter's home, I asked if we could attend Sunday Mass at Ste. Marie Church the next day instead of St. Catherine's. We sat in the center aisle of Sainte Marie church. I was enamored by the incredible beauty of this Gothic style structure. The intricate carving of all the wood that graced the huge altar is indescribable. The stained-glass windows each depicting an apparition of Our Blessed Mother that encircled the church are magnificent. I even found myself staring up at the figures on the ceiling. It was so breathtaking, I was hardly praying. And then it happened! I looked up at the huge stained glass window at the right side of the altar depicting the Annunciation and there it was – huge letters on either side of Mary - EVA and AVE! I nearly jumped up and shouted! That's it! That was God's confirmation for me. I thought, "Our blessed Mother is honored here, the power of the Holy Spirit is alive here, a sign of my angel Eva is here. I'm staying! I'm home!" May I add, I have never seen that Eva – Ave in any other church even to this day.

The next day I called and joined the parish. I also called the priest who heard my confession and asked him if he would see me for spiritual direction. He gave me an appointment right away. (I knew this was another confirmation.)

When I related all this to my children, they were somewhat surprised since I had only been in Manchester two weeks. I assured them I had no doubt that God guided me there. It wasn't long until they also became parishioners.

Life was pretty hectic in the days that followed. I began the refresher course at St. Joseph Hospital in Nashua, NH. It was a grueling schedule, going to school and working nights at the Nursing Home full time. By November 1989, I completed the course and secured my New Hampshire Registered

Professional Nurse license.

I continued working the night shift. Despite the crazy schedule, I actually enjoyed it. I worked with my new friend Martha. It was great becoming acquainted with the licensed nurse aides on the shift. Some of them came to know the power of the Holy Spirit while I worked there. On our breaks, sometimes Martha and I would make it a prayer break. Often when we got off duty, we would race down the hill to Mass at the Cathedral. I always managed to include daily Mass in my day no matter what was going on in my day.

It was sad to see the many patients who never had any visitors. Some families were not present even as death drew near for their family member. They would just leave word as to which funeral director to call when they died. Martha and I often prayed with them as they passed. More than once, I heard Martha whisper in their ear, "don't forget to tell Jesus about us when you see Him." It was really a blessed time.

At the same time, I decided to resume my studies and registered once again at St. Joseph College in Maine. I couldn't seem to let go of the idea that although I was well qualified and had a lot of experience, maybe I should earn a BS. I enjoyed it to a degree. Then I began to experience sleep deprivation as I stayed awake more to study and complete my assignments.

After completing another course, I decided to give up that idea. I couldn't seem to do it all.

I wasn't really sure of what God wanted from me at this point but I was not interested in any ministry. I requested not to work Sundays because it was "family day". I explained to the supervisor that "I didn't move here to be the best nurse in New Hampshire. I came to be near my family and that Sunday was important in our family". They honored my request. Sometimes I would work Sunday night but not often.

XIX
Time Out for Mom

'Honor your Mother...'

In late November of 1991, my mother began to experience serious problems with her foot. The doctor was concerned about her circulation and possibility of gangrene setting in. The family talked about nursing home care for her. I couldn't even conceive of that for her. So after much prayer and discernment, I decided to take a leave from my job and go to Oswego and stay with her to assess the situation. I had to know first-hand that she was unable to stay in her own home. I gave up my condo, took a leave from my job, put my things in storage and went to Oswego to stay with her.

Caring for my Mom was not difficult. She was ambulatory and walked with the aid of a cane. Because it was winter, there was little opportunity to walk outdoors. She already had meals on wheels delivered daily which she was happy with. They accommodated her diabetic diet very well. So I didn't do much cooking. I stayed with her for three months. In that time, I observed how she could manage. She seemed to gain strength and it was decided with the support of family members and health services coming in, she would stay at home. So at the end of three months, I left to return to NH.

My time with my mom bought her another year and a half at home.

When the subject of nursing home care came up again, I was

distraught. I wanted to go to Oswego once again but I didn't know how I could do it. It put me in a difficult financial spot the last time. But I would go if God wanted it. I went to my spiritual director and he prayed with me.

Father said, "I believe God is saying, no, it is not for you to go this time. God has work for you here."

Mom underwent an above the knee amputation and entered the nursing home for rehabilitation. Of course it was with the hope that she would eventually be able to return home. I think everyone was really resigned to the fact that it would not happen that way. Her age was not in her favor for the rigorous rehab required for an above the knee amputation. The family in Oswego visited her regularly and cared for her needs. My children and I went to visit her when we could travel to Oswego. Her vacant home stood just as she left it. I know she was hoping she would go back home after some rehab but it looked unlikely. The family was concerned about her depression.

I had just gotten a new car and Thanksgiving was approaching. I called my sister Eileen and spoke with her about taking Mom home for the holiday. So together we conjured up a plan. I would come to Oswego and pick her up from the nursing home and bring her home and stay with her in her house. She could sleep in her own bed for a night. I would bring her to Eileen and Mike's for Thanksgiving Day. I thought it would help her to see that the house was still there for her. I teased her about checking to see that the boy's (my three brothers) pictures still hung on the living room wall. She loved all nine children but her sons were so very special to her. Deep in my heart, I knew that it would help lift her spirits or be an opportunity to say a final goodbye to the home she so dearly loved. She enjoyed everything. She even slept peacefully without elevating the head of her bed and without oxygen unlike when she was in the nursing home. It was lovely time. I brought her back to the nursing home that night, stayed a bit and told her I loved her as I said goodbye.

I returned to NH on Sunday.

The following Monday, I received the call telling me she died during the night. I was so grieved. Why couldn't God have taken her while I was with her? But no matter what I felt or thought, I was grateful for the weekend. She died November 30, 1993.

XX
A New Opportunity

For we are his handiwork,
created in Christ Jesus for the good works
that God has prepared in advance,
that we should live in them.

Ephesians 2:10

My children seemed concerned about my schedule not being the healthiest arrangement, suggesting I should consider a day job. As God would have it, a part-time nurse that I became acquainted with worked full-time for the State as a Medical Assistant. After discussing with her what her job entailed, I told her to let me know if and when any openings occurred. She assured me that my background certainly qualified me for that kind of position. A few months later, I went through the process of securing the position.

Along with all my experience in social work and nursing, one of the things I had done that added to my qualifications was what I did for my mother. The job opening was in the Home and Community Based Care Unit. On March 25, 1993, I left the Nursing Home to take the job as Medical Assistant for the State of New Hampshire. I really stepped out in faith. Travelling all over a state I knew nothing about was a challenge but I felt equal to the task. God had given me the job. I was sure He would help me.

I enjoyed meeting new people and helping where it was needed. Since I didn't really have much of a social life besides church, my family and the prayer group, I managed the long hours and travel alright. I still had weekend for family so I was pretty content.

I continued to listen for the Lord's guidance. When I first talked to my spiritual director about my goals, etc., I made it clear that I did not move to NH to do ministry. I had enough of all that it involves and didn't feel God prompting me to anything more. He told me God wanted to heal me and it would take time. He was absolutely right.

I did, however, attend the prayer meeting every week. From the very beginning, I believed I heard the Lord say, *"if you continue to use the gift of prophecy in the prayer group, I will multiply the gift in the community."* He certainly did that.

I was invited to serve on the prophetic word ministry at the first Pentecost celebration I attended at Sainte Marie Parish. There were only three invited to share the prophetic word. I felt especially honored. I am extremely grateful to the Lord that I have learned to recognize His voice and I treasure that gift.

Pentecost was a huge celebration with standing room only in the church. We had processed into church praising the Lord with such volume that I'm certain the sound flooded the neighborhood. As I sat on the altar and observed the overflowing pews and balconies and the beautiful flowers and banners everywhere in this magnificent church, I was so moved and overwhelmed; I had to choke back the tears of joy. I

thought to myself, "How on earth did I ever get here?"
I was overwhelmed!

One day after the 5:30 PM Mass, I was chatting with a couple about an upcoming event. Donna said, "We will be attending a healing conference that same week in Rutland, VT given by Francis and Judith MacNutt".
When I heard that, chills went through my body and I said, "Wouldn't I love to hear them speak? I have been praying with my friend and prayer partner back in Utica for them for years because of the turmoil they have endured."

David offered to help arrange an invitation right on the spot. He actually went back into the church hall and made the call. I was almost breathless. I didn't have the money for that and didn't know if I could get vacation time so quickly. David assured me of a scholarship after talking with George Larson. Since the hotel was all booked, Rena Larson arranged for me to stay in a private home with a friend she knew. David and Donna offered me the transportation. Once I secured the vacation time I was on my way. I could hardly believe it.
It was in June 1994 that I attended my first of which would be many "Fishnet" Conferences. It was unforgettable! I felt like I was sitting at the feet of our Lord Jesus the whole time. I wept through most of the teaching and preaching. Added to the

blessings was the amazing spirit-filled preaching of Brennan Manning, a well-known author, speaker and former Franciscan priest. I had many opportunities to receive prayer. I do not have words adequate to convey what that time meant to me. One thing I knew for sure. God willing, I would return again the next year. I even went by myself for a few years. After all these years, I still attend that yearly conference, now known as "Christian Healing Ministries New England".

God continued to heal me many times through these conferences. Our parish prayer meeting had monthly Charismatic Masses which we loved. I served on the Core Leadership Group and continued to use the gift of prophecy in the gatherings. Life in the parish was very active with new ministries growing and conferences offered.

During a holy hour held in the church with the prayer group, God gave me this mental vision and word:
He told me that we should be offering healing prayer at our monthly Charismatic Meetings – that we should be feeding the multitudes not just ourselves. He showed me the altar and the precious blood flowing down from the tabernacle, down the aisle, out the front door of the church and into the streets of the city and beyond into the whole state of NH.

I shared this at the next Core leadership meeting. We began to spread the word that we would offer prayer after the monthly Charismatic Masses and that all Masses would be celebrated in the church and no longer in the school auditorium.

XXI
Called to Pray

"Build the Army"

Although I sometimes prayed with people after Mass, I still was not convinced that I wanted to be involved in healing, still remembering the pain in Utica. Then our parish set up a prayer room in the back of the church and began to offer individual prayer after Sunday Masses and we were asked to pray. I had prayed with my friend John at healing Masses and we seemed to pray well as a team. I agreed to pray with him in the prayer room on Sunday whenever asked.

In June 1996, at a Fishnet conference, while receiving prayer ministry, I asked the Lord what He was asking of me.

I heard Him say, *"Build the Army"*.

My response was, "how?" With my promise to Mari-Beth about *"who will tell them Jesus heals"* ever present in my memory, I was still reluctant to step out of the crowd, so to speak. There is always a price. Scripture tells us, *"When you come to serve the Lord, prepare yourself for trials."*

One thing I was sure of. I would never just step out and begin a healing ministry. I knew that God called me to healing years before and I was obedient and willing and served back in NY. I found myself arguing with God.

First of all, one needs credibility in the church to teach. My past experience accounted for a lot but who was I to do this? Also, approved teaching materials and administrative covering through the parish would be required. Where would I begin? I always saw myself as "the yeast in the dough" and that seemed enough for me. I prayed and prayed.

I decided to ask some friends to gather with me and spend time asking and listening to the Lord. I wanted to know *"God's mind"* on this issue. We gathered in prayer several times and prayed with a tape recorder in the center so we didn't miss anyone's prophetic word. We listened and listened and listened.

In the midst of this time, I received a Christian Healing Ministries newsletter advertising a new thing. They now had made available videos of healing classes by Francis and Judith MacNutt of Christian Healing Ministries in. Jacksonville, FL called the School of Healing Prayer Seminars. Praise the Lord! Teachings done by credible leaders that we could facilitate to learn more about healing. This would enable us to train our pray-ers for ministry in our own community. Was this the answer to my "how" prayer? Maybe.

The more I prayed, the more I was convinced this must be the answer. The Lord had confirmed my date to retire from my position as Medical Assistant for the State of New Hampshire as September 1, so I obeyed and began to make plans. I knew it was going to be a sacrifice. Just like the move to NH, It didn't make sense to other people but that's what I heard. It was going to be tough going living on my meager retirement and social security. Our intercession group confirmed what I was hearing as well.

I conveyed this to my spiritual director who also happened to be the pastor. He listened politely but informed me that there was no money in the budget for a healing ministry. It was a pretty flat no. Now what? I knew that I would only proceed with Father's approval. I know better than to attempt any ministry without the pastor's approval, spiritual covering, spiritual guidance and support. I was stopped in my tracks, so to speak. I did the only thing I knew to do – pray and seek the Lord again. I needed to know what God's mind was on this.

A few months passed. No new words – just the same old ones. I was pretty sure I was on the right track. I just didn't know what to do about it. I felt like I hit a stone wall. So what to do? "Sit down by the stone wall and pray till God removes it or shows me how to leap over it," I thought.
During this time, our parish offered a -four day evening retreat which I attended. Each night we received a prayer card of the holy person being discussed. On one particular night, the

scripture on the back of the card distributed was:

"The Spirit of the Lord is upon me,
because he has anointed me
to bring glad tidings to the poor.
He has sent me to proclaim liberty to captives
and recovery of sight to the blind,
to let the oppressed go free,
and to proclaim a year acceptable to the Lord."
Luke 4: 18-19

That arrested me. "That is the word I need to pray for this ministry," I thought. I shared this with another woman from our group and she agreed to pray it as well.

Every once in a while, a particular memory would fly through my mind. It was something that happened to me when I received the first prophecy I ever got over thirty years ago. It happened during one of my first prayer meetings. We were in a time of waiting to hear the Lord speak in the prayer meeting. I was "a mere babe" in my new growth in the power of the Holy Spirit. On this occasion, as I listened, I felt a tremendous pounding in my chest and heard beautiful words. *"I am in you and you are in me"…..* I thought it was lovely but I didn't understand the pounding and I remained quiet. The next week during the prayer meeting, Father again led us in a time of listening for the prophetic word. This time he added, "If God has given you a word to speak, He may not give you another one until you share the one you have." The same thing happened with the pounding and I heard the same words. Then I heard *"open your mouth and speak it"*. I did and the Lord gave me the rest of the word. And the word was confirmed. The exhortation from Father was the encouragement I apparently needed to speak. That was the beginning of my growth in the gift of prophecy. I like to remember that because I value this gift and don't take it lightly. I always want to be obedient.

I began to learn about this tremendous gift given to encourage and bless God's people. It's not predicting the future in this gift. This is a "now" word to speak. It so encouraged me and even to this day I seldom get many words until the time to speak them. I don't look to the world for much encouragement in growing in this gift but to the Lord and am always obedient to Him and to the magisterium of the church. We know that the effectiveness of the word proclaimed depends on the acceptance of the listener. Therefore, not all words received bear fruit, at least not immediately. I think sometimes God has to do an *"end run"* to get the job done.

At that point in time, our family gathered once a month on Saturday evening to celebrate what we called "Lord's Day Celebration". Family included some close friends we considered extended family. The evening included an hour of praise and worship, sharing a meal and enjoying each other's company. It was our way of opening the Lord's Day. We brought our concerns to the Lord by writing them out on little slips of paper and placing them in a basket during praise and worship, praying over the basket and then burning them later in the fireplace.

During one of these gatherings, I put my concerns about this ministry and the idea of using the School of Healing Prayer Level One as a way to begin to *"build the army"* in the prayer basket. Later in the evening, my friend Martha gave me a check for $100 toward the purchase of the tapes. She said the Lord wanted this and would provide the rest of the cost. Within two weeks I had donations from others and had enough to purchase the tapes.

During my next spiritual direction session with the pastor, I related this whole story of what had transpired. I told him that even though I had the money I would not purchase the tapes without his approval and blessing. I would return the money to the donors if he said no. At which point, he said to me, "I trust you. What would you need from me?" I knew there would be no budget offered. I asked for a classroom, a TV/VCR and his spiritual support which he granted. I assured him I would keep him apprised of everything. That was just the beginning.

Our healing prayer ministry began offering the School of Healing Prayer Seminar Level One published by Christian Ministries, Inc. Jacksonville, FL. When we received the tapes, I was delighted to see that the scripture on the cover was Luke 4:18-19. God is so good to confirm his word and guide us along the way.

Our first group completed the seminar in March 1997. Thus our Sainte Marie Healing Prayer Ministry began. Level One was the only series available for a while so we continued to offer it with great success in participation. The more people who were trained through these courses, the more prayer ministers were available to serve at the many conferences and gatherings that were offered during the following years.

Our need for a permanent classroom was evident. Father offered us a place on the third floor of the Hevey School building on Cartier Street, a part of the Sainte Marie campus. It was greatly in need of renovation. The restoration project for our classroom was another gift from God. I told Father that I put all into the hands of our friend and fellow prayer minister, Johnyne. Besides being a wonderful medical doctor, she was a generous giver and hard worker with an amazing eye for interior decorating and a love for the arts. Except for the floor refinishing, which she paid to have done, she did everything else herself. She painted, hung curtains, and provided furniture. Even the artwork she hung were reproductions of religious photos she took on pilgrimage in Europe that she enlarged and framed. Father provided some additional tables and chairs for us. It was completed with a few of our own touches and ready for class. Johnyne absorbed all the cost with the condition that her contributions remain anonymous. We were all overwhelmed at her generosity but honored her request for anonymity until she died. After her death, I thought it fitting to frame her photograph with a verse I wrote about her and hung it in the classroom.

Since I had over twenty years experience as a registered professional nurse as well as twenty-three years as a social worker, I could see the value of this healing prayer knowledge for the professions. I inquired with Christian Healing Ministries regarding continuing education credits. I was informed that it had to be done in each state and I was welcome to proceed in New Hampshire if I wished, which I did. It was a long process and a lot of work and expense. After completing all the necessary forms and meeting all the requirements, we were given approval by the State Nursing Board to award Continuing Education Units for Level One.

Soon the School of Healing Prayer Seminar Level Two was published and many of those who completed Level One were delighted to take the Level Two that was offered. In time, we also received approval to award CEUs[2] for Level Two and years later for Level Three, as well. Over time, the cost for securing the State approval kept increasing until it became no longer cost effective so we abandoned the idea of awarding credits. However, we continued to offer the levels with great success.

Our classes were enthusiastic to learn to pray for healing. Many came from other parishes and other parts of the state. It was amazing to see how many practicing Catholics and other Christians did not know that it is possible to pray for healing for ourselves and for one another. Since the teachings are ecumenical, we have had students from other denominations as well. The ministry continues to offer these classes and those who complete the course serve as prayer ministers at healing Masses, conferences, small group ministries and individual and soaking prayer.

We continue to encourage everyone in our classes to attend the annual Christian Healing Ministries gathering in New England

---

[2] *Continuing Education Units*

every June to learn and experience more in healing. There is always more to learn and experience. I believe it is important to attend a spiritual renewal conference or retreat at least once a year for our own personal renewal and spiritual growth, especially if one is in active ministry.

I have attended CHM's Fishnet (which is now known as CHM, New England) since 1994. Two of those years, when my health made it impossible for me to travel, I attended through live-streaming the conference. There is always more to learn from others in the healing prayer ministry. We have been privileged to hear many well known speakers including Francis and Judith MacNutt, over the years at these spirit-filled gatherings, with numerous opportunities to receive prayer.

XXII
Listening for His Word and Sharing the Wealth

Your word is a lamp for my feet,
a light for my path.

Psalm 119:105

S ince the very first day that I heard God's word to "*Build the Army*", I have tried to listen carefully to God's word to me and through others committed to our ministry. With the first focus group that was formed to try to discern God's plan for our ministry, I have always taken His word seriously even if it has not yet been manifested. I realize sometimes God speaks a word that does not manifest for years.

During one of our focus group gatherings on August 22, 1997 God spoke these words:

"Some write a tune and the notes disappear. Some write a symphony and it plays over and over and never dies."

Then God showed one of the women a mental vision. It was a musical score that God was holding up keeping the G clef in place. As the notes were written on the score, something was trying to erase the notes but they kept re-appearing and the Lord said,

"Some may try to erase the notes but I continue to provide the notes for the music and I hold the rhythm for the symphony."

Also, *"Man's song lasts only a short time – God's song lasts forever. God works in unity, harmony, love and joy."*

As our ministry grew, we tried to bring awareness of healing to our community in many ways. We collaborated with the

Women of Mary[3] and together hosted conferences at Ste. Marie Church. We invited speakers such as: Susan Stanford-Rue, PhD and Rev. Francis Pompei, OFM, as well as Neil and Janet Lozano, who introduced their Unbound Healing Ministry.

When the prayer group disbanded, Ste. Marie Healing Ministry took over the monthly healing Mass to insure its continuance. We provided the prayer ministers and invited different priests from all over NH to celebrate with us each month. Soon the word spread over the state. Many priests now offer healing Masses in their own parishes which is wonderful for the people of New Hampshire. Our own Generational Healing Mass which we began to offer as part of the School of Healing Prayer Seminars is now offered in other parishes.

It still amazes me that there are so many faithful believers who do not know or believe that Jesus still heals today. I believe that the healing power of Jesus Christ especially among the laity is one of the greatest tools of evangelization the church has at its disposal.

I believe we are a faithful church but also very needy. There are

---

[3] *The* **Women of Mary** *meet once a month for rosary, meditation, Mass, teaching and fellowship. The primary focus of the Women of Mary is to become closer to Jesus Christ through the prayerful intercession of Mary.*

many who suffer silently because they don't know that Jesus wants to heal them. Some may not be healed physically but experience great emotional healing and spiritual peace.

It is also a great ecumenical tool. Praying with other believing Christians for healing in the name of Jesus Christ has been one of the joys of my life. The great thing about this ministry is the total acceptance we have for one another. We share the things we have in common. It is so great to see people healed.

Although the healing power of Jesus Christ is alive in our midst, there is much more to be done. One has only to hear the daily news to discern the great need for inner healing and generational healing.

As Christians, we are called to evangelization: to share the Good News of Jesus Christ. I continue to believe that we are called to *listen, love and pray* for those in need and when Jesus heals them, they will shout their witness from the rooftops – that's evangelization!"

XXIII
Again, Lord? Really?

*Jesus Christ is the same
yesterday, today, and forever.*

Hebrews 13:8

Christmas holidays! My favorite time of year! I love all the sights, sounds and smells of Christmas. Our homes are filled with the aroma of Christmas trees and holly and wonderful smells of Christmas baking wafting from our kitchens. Christmas carols are playing wherever you are. Everyone is in preparation mode. People seem to be kinder, more thoughtful and generous. There is a spirit of joyful expectation and excitement everywhere and even a special feeling of hope that seems to fill the air.

We were anticipating a wonderful gathering of family and friends for a Christmas Open House Celebration at the Dunn's. Kelly and Peter were hosting the party and we were all planning to attend. Most of our immediate family lives here in New Hampshire but the Kunkels would be traveling here from Vermont.

The following is Kim's journey, written by her.

Kim's Journey

By Kimberly A. M. Kunkel

December 28, 2011

December 28, 2011! Little did I know how much this date would someday mean to me. As I look back, this day was incredibly painful. However, two years later this date would mark something wonderful!

Lee and I were vacillating about attending Kelly and Peter Dunn's Christmas party. Lee is in the investment business and year's end is extremely busy for him. He is always home to celebrate Christmas from December 24 to December 28. Then it's back to work for a few days to help clients who need to make yearend changes. The timing of the Dunn's party in New Hampshire wasn't going to work for him this year. I was disappointed Lee couldn't make the trip but I was excited to see Mom and the "sisters". Kristin and Brian would be traveling together as they had their own plans for New Years Eve. John and Noelle would be traveling from Noelle's family home in Nashua to the Dunn's. Unfortunately, Joshua and Kyle were unable to make it but I was still looking forward to the party.

I was enjoying the drive from Vermont on this beautiful sunny day when my cell phone rang. I didn't recognize the number but I answered it quickly. The caller identified herself as a nurse from the University of Vermont Medical Center.

"Can you talk?" she asked.

Well, this doesn't sound good, I thought.

She proceeded to explain that the breast biopsy I had taken before Christmas came back positive, not just in one spot but in two.

Actually I wasn't really shocked. As I recalled the day of the biopsy, I thought I caught a glimmer of sadness in the doctor's eyes. I kept that to myself but suddenly remembered it clearly as she spoke.

"Do you have any questions?" the nurse asked.

"Questions?" I thought. "Yes. Too many but none that I could formulate into complete sentences at that moment". We ended the call.

Suddenly I saw my daughter Kristin and son Brian whizzing by, passing me in the outside lane. I wanted to call her and tell her to slow down. What I really wanted was to slow down the flow of thoughts and feelings that were beginning to percolate inside of me.

The reality hit me and I knew I had to call Lee. I felt devastated and Lee has always been my rock. I don't remember what I said but Lee was calm and calmed me down. He reminded me that God is in charge and that all would be well. After a long emotional conversation, we decided to consult with my primary care physician as well as our friends in the medical profession to identify the best experts available in this field including a trusted breast surgeon to coordinate all of my care.

As I drove, I realized I was almost to Dunn's and was not ready to see my kids. I needed to compose myself a little more. I called Mom. I knew that I could stop at her house, pull myself together and just pray with her. I'm sure that phone call was not easy for my mother – *another daughter with cancer!* That is a call no parent ever wants to receive.

I spent some time with Mom. We prayed and I made some calls to schedule some appointments that would start the journey. After a while, I felt like I could tackle telling our children and my sisters and brother-in-law. At least most of them were in the same place at the same time. Taking a deep breath, I headed over to the Dunn's.

Reactions were all across the board but I sure felt everyone's love. I made it through the first step, called Lee again – one of many calls I would make that night and got ready for the party.

I knew I would have to tell Joshua and Kyle the next day but for now I was fine.

The Christmas party was lovely and lively. And as God would have it, one of the guests was the family pastor, Father Moe Larochelle. After being told of the situation, he offered to pray. We found a spot amidst the party and he ministered the Sacrament of the Sick and prayed for healing. Father Moe smiled and said, "I guess that is why I am here! Who knew?"

Now I was sure that God was in charge.

The days ahead were filled with appointments, plans, research and sometimes just chaos. Through it all, Lee and I were at peace and knew that God was guiding us.

The consensus of the physicians was that I would need a mastectomy and reconstructive surgery. Because two physicians would be required, the surgery could not be scheduled until February 10, 2012. The long wait allowed me the time that I needed to prepare. I put things in order at work and began to intensify my daily workouts to get my body ready for the long surgery and recovery period. I knew I needed to be in very good health in order to tackle this.

February 10, 2012

I awoke to rhythmic beeping sounds, with a nurse checking my heart rate. She was concerned that it was a bit fast but I felt fine. Lee came in looking relieved but a bit worried. I wanted to know exactly what the surgeons had told him but first he wanted to be sure I was ready to have that discussion. The cancer had spread. Three lymph nodes had been removed and one was "involved". I knew that meant chemotherapy and radiation would probably be prescribed.

My first response was, "Well, at least I won't have to worry about how to wear my hair for the weddings!"

Two of our sons, Josh and John were to be married this year and our family was so excited about the upcoming celebrations. I don't know if anyone thought my comment was funny but I was feeling God's peace and I knew I had to leave it all up to Him.

John and Brian had been with Lee all day. Josh was on the "red eye" flight from San Diego to be with us. Kristin, who was in graduate school at Lemoyne College in Syracuse, NY, was driving to Vermont, stopping on the way to pick up Kyle in Albany. Noelle was coming straight from work and our entire family would soon be gathered together again. I remember feeling so grateful for my faith and my family that supports each other in good times and in bad.

Spring 2012

Our family huddled together in the days and weeks to follow. My surgery had been pretty extensive, requiring eight weeks of recovery time. After consulting with physicians, family members, much research and prayer, it was clear that I should undergo four months of chemotherapy. Radiation treatment was also suggested but after extensive research on my specific medical condition, I decided to forego radiation in exchange for an intensive program of nutrition and exercise.

At the end of March, the chemotherapy treatments began. By the day after Easter, I had lost all of my hair. Every two weeks, my sister Kelly and my mother came from Manchester to Vermont to support me through the chemo. Kelly and I would go into the treatment room for two hours while Mom took up her self-assigned post in the waiting room to pray and intercede. Kelly and I would discuss the upcoming weddings and all the news and generally be silly, as sisters can be. This experience, though difficult went better that I ever expected. I know that it is because of all the prayer, Lee and the family praying and all our friends plus Mom in the waiting room. I remember when my sister Mari-Beth was receiving chemotherapy at the ORU City of Faith in Tulsa; she said that having people around her in prayer made all the difference. She was right.

Summer 2012

On June 29, 2012, our family celebrated the first of our children's weddings. John and Noelle were married in a lovely church in Pepperell, MA complete with our Bishop's blessing. It was a beautiful celebration. I wore my wig and felt so happy and blessed just to be there.

In mid-July, Kelly and I donned ridiculous hats to wear to the clinic for my final chemo treatment. Another milestone reached! Praise God!

Fall 2012

On September 22, 2012, we celebrated Josh and Kyle's wedding, complete with our Albany pastor and friend Father Doyle officiating. It was another beautiful celebration.

My hair was about an inch long and I was sick of wearing wigs and scarves. Lee encouraged me to leave the wig in the car at the last minute. I decided to brave it with my new "natural look". Everyone said I looked great. I'm pretty sure they were all being kind but I felt good. It was another amazing wedding and I felt so grateful to God and to my family that I could be there to enjoy it.

2013

Fast forward to 2013. It was a steady recovery after all the surgery and chemotherapy. It took over a year to feel like myself again. I worked hard with my primary care physician to develop and maintain a program of nutrition and exercise. Many days I "leaned heavy" on the Lord to get me through.

In 2013 I was blessed again! There I was walking down the aisle as mother of the bride. Our beautiful daughter Kristin and Mark were married at the historic St. Anne's Shrine Isle in LaMotte, VT, on the first sunny day after weeks of rain! As in the other two weddings, beautiful and moving music was provided by our youngest son, Brian, which gave us all another moment to shed a few more tears. Lee and I felt especially blessed to celebrate their wedding at this holy shrine of the saint for whom I am named Kimberly Ann.

At the end of the year, on December 28, 2013, the same date as my diagnosis in 2011, Lee and I welcomed our first grandchild, Caleb Michael into our family.

October 2016

It has been almost five years since that initial diagnosis. I've just completed my annual round of check-ups and tests. I am healthy and so grateful to the Lord and to my family for all their love and support. Lee and I are enjoying our families and watching them grow. We have three more grandchildren on the way and are looking forward to all the God has for all of us. God is good!

Kimberly Ann Moore Kunkel

XXIV
To God Be The Glory!

And whatever you do, in word or in deed,
do everything in the name of the Lord Jesus,
giving thanks to God the Father through him.

Col 3:17

I am truly grateful to God for everyday and try to accept all that comes with gratitude. We never know what tomorrow may bring, but it is wonderful to know He has all in the palm of His hand, never leaves us and always has a plan. We just have to "hear and obey".

It's easy to be thankful and joyful when things are going well but when all goes awry, not so much. However, I have learned that expression that is credited to Abraham Lincoln is true. We can be "as happy as we make up our minds to be". There is always something to be happy about. We learned that even through the suffering.

No matter what is thrown into our paths, we know God is always there. I am grieved when I hear of suicides and those who give up on life. There is always healing available. God is still in the "healing business".

In this book, I have tried to convey our true story of how we learned to lean on God and trust in his mercy. So many questions are evident? How is it that Mari-Beth died of cancer at such a young age with everything to live for? Why did God arrest the growth of Teresa's fast-growing tumor and allow it to be surgically removed successfully in the time she asked for and then found to be benign? Why was Kimberly Ann subjected to the long suffering of major surgery, chemotherapy and all that goes with rehabilitation and then healed? These questions and more have been asked and pondered on over the years. And last, but not least – why did God ask me to walk this road as well? Honestly, I have no idea.

This I do know and I can clearly attest to. God never left us then and is still with us now. I have learned that suffering does change people. It changed us and those around us. We are taught that we will encounter suffering in the world and to embrace the cross in our lives. I believe we do that by trusting in the Lord, being who we are, doing our best and praying that He use it for our own good and the good of others. I believe God will heal us and He does. In our healing prayer ministry, we listen, love and pray expecting God to provide the answer.

As a nurse for many years, I can testify to the marvels of modern science and the miracles worked through the medical profession. We live in an amazing age.

In the book of Sirach, chapter 38:1-15, one can read what we are told to do when we are sick. First we pray to the Lord who heals. Then we seek the physician and his recommendations. We are encouraged to give up our faults and cleanse our hearts. In our Catholic church, we can seek the Sacrament of Reconciliation and the Sacrament for the Sick, and in many places there are healing Masses available. In most Christian denominations, there are prayer ministries available to pray for your decision-making as well as for your healing and peace. We may want to do our own research as well. In this day and time, we have access to the internet for information and may also seek more than one opinion. We can then make a more informed decision and put all in the hands of the physicians we have chosen and for whom we also pray. Scripture tells us that recovery may lie in the hands of the physician for they too pray to God for success.

Today, as opposed to years ago, a patient's wishes or opinion regarding choice of treatment is taken into consideration in the decision-making process by the medical profession. Patients are no longer treated as hostile or uncooperative if they ask questions or resist some types of treatment. I believe great strides have been made in this area.

I believe that healing prayer is effective in all the steps of the process. It can bring peace into the scenario and encourage the confidence of the patient. In our healing prayer ministry, we include prayer for the doctors, nurses and the health provider's team whenever someone comes to us that is in that situation.

The Holy Spirit is always available when we call for help. In our immediate family, we have learned to pray for each other. We know that to "lay hands" on one another and pray for our needs always bears fruit. I believe that we are all called to minister to our own families in our own "domestic churches".

I am very grateful for the power of the Holy Spirit that was awakened in me and my family in experiencing the Baptism of the Holy Spirit through the Charismatic Renewal. For those who still have not unwrapped the Charismatic gifts in your life, I offer a simple prayer that you will, as God leads you.

Praise the Lord!

Epilogue
Born to Shine

You are the light of the world.
A city set on a mountain cannot be hidden.
Nor do they light a lamp and then
put it under a bushel basket;
it is set on a lampstand,
where it gives light to all in the house.
Just so, your light must shine before others,
that they may see your good deeds
and glorify your heavenly Father.

Matthew 5:14-16

God calls us to be a light in the darkness of our world. I believe we can do this by being who we are in Jesus Christ. In some small way, our faith lived well may ignite the faith in those around us.

Over the years I have received many words from friends and relatives of fond memories of Mari-Beth. I treasure them all and it warms my heart to remember.

The following was written by a dear friend of Mari-Beth's and shared in his parish on the Thanksgiving after her death.

> *Faith is a funny thing. Most of us don't even know we have it and we're never thankful for it. At Thanksgiving, we look at our lives and we're thankful for the food, our homes, our cars, our families, or else we're sad because we don't have as much as we think we should. We never take the time to thank God for one of his greatest gifts to us as Christians: our faith in Him, the faith that can see us through any problems we may have.*
>
> *A friend of mine died this year. She was twenty-six years old. Mari-Beth found out she had cancer two days after she had given birth to her first child. Nine months later she was dead. In that short period of time, Mari-Beth taught me more about faith than I had learned in my entire life. Rather than dwell on the terrible disease that was growing inside her, Mari-Beth chose to put herself in the Lord's hands and live as happily as she could. Some people, myself included were turned off by the expressions of her faith that often found their way into her conversation. But Mari-Beth thanked God every day for the faith He had given her to see her through this terrible time. And that terrible time became a little less for those of us around because of her strength.*

Two days before she died, Mari-Beth's husband, Dan, and two friends gathered around her hospital bed to celebrate Mass. The priest, an old friend of Mari-Beth's, asked her if there was any song she would like them to sing. Mari- Beth chose this song, -- "Be not afraid, I go before you always, come follow me and I will give you rest".

Father Doyle spoke of this special Mass at Mari-Beth's funeral and I remember feeling the joy that understanding can bring. This joy came from knowing that I could also share the gift Mari-Beth had been so grateful for; the gift of faith.

Thanksgiving means something a little different to me now. I'll still go home and eat turkey and watch football and talk with my family. But I know now that if I should lose it all, I would still have everything. I would still have the gift of faith. I'm thankful I can finally see that. I know Mari-Beth is too.

By Dennis Tompkins